By the time I finished reading *Leave the Dogs at Home,* I felt sure I was holding a future classic. The best thing about Claire Arbogast, besides her wonderful writing, is her hard-headed sense of intimacy and her stubborn determination to live a life of love – whatever craziness and jury-rigging that might require from the heart.

Bob Shacochis, author of *The Woman Who Lost Her Soul*

In this stunning debut, Claire Arbogast infuses death with life, giving readers both the gut-punch of grief as well as the warmth of a life well lived. Candid, powerful, and unrelenting ... Arbogast's pain becomes our pain, and her love becomes our love.

B. J. Hollars, author of *This Is Only a Test*

Claire Arbogast rewrites the stages of grief in this raw, sometimes unsettling, always compelling memoir that takes us backward and forward in time from the moment her intense, complicated husband is diagnosed with terminal cancer. *Leave the Dogs at Home* challenges the conventional wisdom about love, marriage, loss, survival, and grace in ways that are bound to make you think about your own life.

Barbara Shoup, author of *Looking for Jack Kerouac*

Leave the Dogs at Home mines the messy, graceful territory of life lived in the midst of upheaval; the roughness and tenderness of it all. Sharp and engaging, this beautiful memoir invites us to think about resilience and reconnection with the strongest parts of Self.

Beth Lodge-Rigal, Creative Director,
Women Writing for (a) Change

Leave the Dogs at Home is a memoir about Adults and their very
real lives. Claire and Jim take nearly a lifetime to find their marriage
only to discover Jim has terminal cancer. But this is not so much a
book about grief as it is about love. Readers will share that love and
arrive at the end both stronger and wiser.

Jesse Lee Kercheval, author of
Space: A Memoir and *My Life as a Silent Movie*

Life, just as a garden, does not have to be perfect and neat to be
complete. *Leave the Dogs at Home* serves as a prime example of how
a humble experience in the outdoors can come to our aid in times of
need and healing.

Bruce W. Bytnar, Boxerwood Nature Center and Woodland Garden

Claire Arbogast's deeply moving memoir records with honesty and
clarity how she managed to move forward with her life despite the
death of her husband. Her story beautifully depicts the aftermath of
deep, personal loss.

Carrol Krause, author of *Showers Brothers Furniture Company:
The Shared Fortunes of a Family, a City, and a University*

This very personal memoir is a gift of insightful reflection on how
weathering difficult situations and transitions can help us grow and
transform and blossom again. The vivid imagery and flowing words
were a healing balm. Claire Arbogast has had the courage to find her
voice, her true being, and share it.

Gwen Bottoms, Aging to Sage-ing Facilitator

Leave the Dogs at Home

break away books

INDIANA UNIVERSITY PRESS

Bloomington & Indianapolis

Leave *the* Dogs *at* Home

a memoir

CLAIRE S. ARBOGAST

This book is a publication of

INDIANA UNIVERSITY PRESS
Office of Scholarly Publishing
Herman B Wells Library 350
1320 East 10th Street
Bloomington, Indiana 47405 USA

iupress.indiana.edu

The paper used in this publication
meets the minimum requirements of
the American National Standard for
Information Sciences – Permanence of
Paper for Printed Library Materials,
ANSI Z39.48–1992.

Manufactured in the
United States of America

*Library of Congress
Cataloging-in-Publication Data*

Arbogast, Claire S.
  Leave the dogs at home : a memoir /
Claire S. Arbogast.
    pages cm. – (Break away books)
    Includes bibliographical references.
    ISBN 978-0-253-01719-2 (pb : alk.
paper) – ISBN 978-0-253-01721-5 (eb)
  1. Arbogast, Claire S. 2. Cancer –
Patients – United States – Biography.
3. Cancer – Patients – Family
relationships – United States.
4. Caregivers – United States –
Biography. I. Title.
    RC265.6.A73A3 2015
    362.19699'40092 – dc23
    [B]
                              2015002083

1 2 3 4 5   20 19 18 17 16 15

FOR ALL THOSE WHO LOVE AND GRIEVE
IMPERFECTLY IN WEEDY LIVES

Contents

Acknowledgments

This book would not exist if not for the willing and gracious support of many. Thanks to Boxerwood Nature Center and Woodland Garden in Lexington, Virginia, for providing the freedom and whimsy that spurred the writing of this book. Also thanks to Patti Reum and the now closed Bear Mountain Farm and Wilderness Retreat in Virginia for the simple log cabin and brilliant starry nights where the writing began. And to Dallas Stafford for talking me into buying the timeshare at Hacienda del Mar in Cabo San Lucas, Mexico, where I sat writing during many sunny Februarys.

The 2009 Ropewalk Writer's Conference provided a scholarship to the Master's Class that resulted in my introduction to author and mentor Bob Shacochis and ultimately to Gail Hochman of Brandt & Hochman Literary Agents Inc.; both of them were instrumental in early drafts. The 2009 Jason Sheppard Greer and Lucy Kim Greer Foundation for the Arts grant sustained me during pivotal moments of the manuscript development. Bloomington's Writing for (a) Change and the Writers Guild both provided an encouraging community of writers who helped launch and relaunch the book in moments of floundering.

Thank you to Indiana University Press for reviving the Break Away Book series, especially to editor Michael Martone for his honing guidance and to sponsoring editor Linda Oblack, whose encouragement began in a parking lot.

Acknowledgments

Many people questioned, pushed, and invigorated me. Thanks to Crystal Wilkinson for very early impetus and to Nancy Long for very late impetus. Special thanks go to those who persisted beyond the pale of obligation: Carole Clark, Ayn Todd, Lauren Bryant, Michele Pollack, Susan Fernandes, Susan Moke, and Mary Peckham.

Leave the Dogs at Home

The Fullness

We didn't live together until Jim started dying, but that wasn't the plan.

It was unseasonably warm for November; the first icy fingers of winter 2004 momentarily unclenched when I took the final turn of my long commute onto the southern Indiana country road. It was dark already, and I'd been focused on taking off my pointy-toed shoes, heating up the pot of chicken vegetable soup, and prioritizing my weekend chores when I saw an unexpected bright white light shining through the pines. I turned in to the driveway to discover the glaring halogen spotlights mounted on the front of the pole barn shining onto Jim's pickup, which was backed up to the pale blue metal building. Every light was on and intensity spilled into the night through the two open overhead doors.

Gawking as I slowly drove by the barn, I pulled into the garage. As I got out, our black mutt dogs, Lila and Diggity, burst in from the night to dance dog hellos and to pull me across the broad, black asphalt lot to the pole barn. My tight suit and heels wanted to go the opposite direction, toward dinner and house slippers, but that would have to wait.

When I had left in the morning for work, the barn had been empty except for lawn mowers and leftover fencing. My shovels, tiller, and tomato cages were stored out back in the garden shed. The pole barn had always been reserved for Jim. Now hulking equipment – saws, a drill press, and grinders – created an industrial walkway that channeled me, through darting dogs, to the enclosed workshop he had built inside. The thick wooden double doors leading into the workshop were ajar, and Jim was sitting in his green swivel chair surrounded by a jumble of hammers, screwdrivers, files, and a thicket of cardboard boxes. The blazing lights caught his almost auburn, hopefully combed-over hair. A sheen of exhaustion coated his washed-out face.

"Why didn't you tell me you were moving in?" I asked in amazement. "I would have helped you. You could have waited until the weekend."

"I didn't need help," he said dismissively.

He heaved himself up from the chair as I wandered out of the workshop into the depths of the pole barn, taking in the change. Behind the workshop, towering shelves were packed with an assemblage of contraptions, renditions of wall-size terrariums, and every model of the Dog-Proof Cat Feeder Jim had ever built.

"This is the invention museum." Jim propped his long, lean frame against a sturdy end post. "A monument to a lifetime wasted on foolishness," he said with a wry smile flitting across his full lips. Bemusement flickered briefly in his tired eyes.

I walked over to him and slipped my hand in his, bringing it to my mouth to kiss his scraped knuckles, then running my fingertips over his calluses. "I can't believe you did this all today and all by yourself." I turned and leaned my back against his chest and looked up. He wrapped his long arms around me. "What's up there?" I asked, pointing to the dozens of boxes in the storage area above the workshop.

"My books."

I drew a sharp breath. These books had lined his study from floor to ceiling in the house he was leaving. Books were the starting points for galloping conversations that had sustained long walks in the woods, cross-country driving, and secluded snowy afternoons over all the years between us. I knew his library as well as my own. In the middle of some developing debate, I could walk to his bookshelf and pull out his copy of Edward O. Wilson's *Consilience: The Unity of Knowledge* and turn to any number of points. I had that book on my bookshelf as well, but our collections didn't match book-for-book. He wasn't just putting his books up there, twelve feet overhead in boxes; he was stowing away half of my reference library too.

You think you know someone, maybe not everything, but some things. I had been sure Jim would always be surrounded by books; it was an ingrained part of him. "You don't need your books?" I said as nonchalantly as possible, twisting to the side to see his face.

"I decided to switch things around," Jim said, releasing his arms from me. "Things that used to be in boxes – you know, stuff like the carvings Dad brought back from Africa after the war, plates and bowls from my time in Vietnam, shells from when we used to dive in the Caribbean – are now on the shelves that used to hold books. I can always change my mind if I want to. If I need some old book, I can just come up here and get it."

"But won't the books mildew in the barn?" I protested, worry tightening just under my skin with the discomfort I found in this jarring shift away from what I had thought to be one of life's little certainties – that these books would always be handy. I would look back at this as blind stupidity on my part, a regretful shallowness that I couldn't see he was bravely making a fresh start.

"They'll be fine," said Jim with a disappointed sternness I didn't understand.

"Do you want some soup?" I asked, hoping to divert the unexpected direction of things.

"No. I've eaten. I want a shower. I'm going to bed." Jim walked away from me and started switching off the lights. As the barn fell dim, I hit the overhead door opener and called the dogs. The three of us jogged out together as the door ratcheted down over our heads; Jim had disappeared ahead toward the house in the dark. He was headed downstairs to his bed. He had finally moved in.

It had taken us twenty-seven years to agree on living together. Over the decades we'd been casual friends, good friends, friends with benefits, friends without benefits, hardly friends at all, happy lovers, bored lovers, vacationing lovers, cruel lovers – every kind of a lover that two people could be who were unable to completely commit or completely split up.

I was in my mid-twenties when Jim and I became friends, forty when we got serious, and had turned fifty-four when we got married earlier this year and now at this moment when he moved in. Our relationship never came close to matching the Hollywood version of romance of two people falling madly in love and merging into one inseparable being with hearts beating in unison.

In fact, we were the most unlikely of lovers. Jim was a reclusive inventor who, until his retirement this year, had hidden out in a factory job. I wore suits and schmoozed around in public relations and advertising. He had been a marine. I had been a war protester. He ate meat almost exclusively. I edged on being vegetarian. He drank beer from cans. I drank beer from bottles. We used to say that we had absolutely nothing in common.

Of course that was our lie. There was an unspoken, undefined, irresistible thing between us that we could not deny or escape – a mystical gold cord that linked us solar plexus to solar plexus. The truth we never faced was how we relied on each other, that I, with my hopeless optimism, was the perfect yin to his yang of cynical pessimism. He was the steady current in my changing life. I was the fresh air in his fixed routine. Either of us without the other was one hand clapping.

Inside the house I kicked off my shoes, unfastened the binding waistband of my skirt, and laid my jacket over the arm of the couch. My cat, Cirrus, meowed her welcome and followed me to the kitchen. The dogs curled up nearby. I leaned on the open refrigerator door, staring immobile at the pot of chicken veggie soup, letting the cool calm the flush of the unexpected turn of the evening.

I don't know how long I stood there hanging off the open door listening to the new, eerie sound of the shower running downstairs. I was almost too tired and distracted to move as I thought about what led to us to buy this house more than two years ago. This house where I had lived upstairs, with a vacant downstairs, until today.

It was a bi-level ranch on a little more than two almost-flat acres about ten miles west of Bloomington, not a place I would have chosen on my own. I thought it had an underlying tacky-trailer character. The land was all fields converted to lawn, terracing up twenty feet in elevation to a pasture plateau. The pasture was set against a neighboring hill of rough scrub woods full of spiky catbriers, thorny multiflora roses, old refrigerators, car parts, and broken glass. To one side was a wetland; across the road were acres of horse pasture and a riding club stable.

I would have preferred a chunk of pristine, parklike woods with no lawn to mow, next to the national forest on the other side of town or down by Lake Monroe, or a low-maintenance place in Bloomington within walking distance to the downtown restaurants and shops. But the land's openness warmed Jim's northern Indiana flatlander's heart, and he was the one who often found it more difficult to adapt, so I agreed. The floor plan was perfect for us: two levels of independent living – one for him and one for me. There was a big kitchen, and my upstairs half was open and flooded with sunlight, with panoramic views of woods, the wetland, and grazing horses. I could deal with it. I could improve it. I could put in a huge, sweeping garden.

We were in a slump when we made the decision to live together, ready to abandon our affair as eternally insufficient and unwieldy. But just as we were in the final stages of rearranging ourselves as friends without benefits, we suddenly turned the opposite direction and resolved to buy this house together. Out of the blue, something made us continue together. It was like a smoldering that mysteriously flares up just when you think the fire is out.

I finally roused myself to ladle some cold soup into a bowl and heated it in the microwave. I poured myself a glass of wine and sat on the bar stool by the kitchen counter, the bowl on the single placemat that was always there. Cirrus jumped up onto the empty stool next to me, as usual, and the dogs roused, alert to possible dinner scraps coming.

I remembered how we had told ourselves it was a practical thing to do, an unassuming nod toward aging. Instead of breaking up, we'd have one lawn and one set of utilities. Someone to notice if one of us fell and couldn't get up. We had joked about installing traffic lights in the stairwell. Green – you can come; red – stay away; yellow – be careful. If we'd had that light, I would have switched it to yellow, but Jim probably would have had it already red.

I had moved into the upper level of the house thinking he would quickly follow and fill in the lower level with his handmade furniture and books. But it didn't happen.

Strange as it sounds, the previous March we had gotten married. It was another pragmatic twist to our complicated situation. We did it for health insurance. He was retiring. If I was on his policy, I could retire early – in six years – without having to wait for Medicare, so we could go on long vacations before he got too old to be any fun. We might not have proven ourselves capable of a traditional relationship, but we had vacations down pat. Still, he hadn't moved in.

Soup eaten almost unnoticed, I poured myself more wine and walked to the long stretch of living room windows looking out into the darkness that hid the pole barn. Jim had said he couldn't move in until he built a workshop in the barn but then went about the task at only glacial speed. Granted, it was a big project – an enclosed, insulated room with its own heat and air conditioning. He had to completely rewire the whole barn, reroute the water supply, line walls of the barn with shelves to hold his inventions.

Our back-and-forth about when he might move in was as stubborn as a cocklebur on socks. "Any idea when you might be finished with the workshop and move in?" I had asked a gazillion increasingly annoyed times.

"In the fullness," he had answered a gazillion unyielding times back. *In the fullness of time,* meaning some distant point in the future.

It was true; he couldn't move in until the workshop was done. Jim and his shop were inseparable – unlike us. He would steal moments or wake in the middle of the night to tinker with his latest invention like some people pull out a guitar or pick up a crochet project, or like how I might revise a garden plan. A chunk of his mind was always churning to solve a tricky problem that was on the workbench in his cramped basement shop. Taking a space from a drafty nothing inside the barn and converting it into his dream place to work was an act of unmitigated magnitude, trumping the fact that his delays hurt and embarrassed me. I guessed that he wished he could back out. I schemed about how I might.

I closed the heavy drapes to cover the wall of windows, sealing off the dropping outdoor temperature, and picked up my journal. I needed to mark this moment. "Less than festive," I wrote. I guessed that this was the fullness. But it didn't seem like fullness.

Instead of feeling elated to have Jim settling in downstairs with the workshop completed, I was wildly desperate. For everything was being jerked up out of the ground with the vigor you'd take to a patch of pigweed in the tomatoes. What had spurred Jim's workshop completion was terror. Three weeks earlier he'd had the upper lobe of his cancerous left lung removed.

This was not part of the plan.

2

Survivor

Unable to sleep, I sat in the darkened house until the middle of the night with Cirrus in my lap. The dogs had given up on me and wandered off to the bedroom. I was unable to imagine clearly what might come, my Jimless future. The last few weeks churned before me in the hushed house.

Jim had hid his lung cancer from me for months. The spot on his lung, mistaken at first for a blood clot, had been found in July. He confessed to me in October. He probably would have never told me, except the surgery to remove his lung would be too hard to hide.

Once Jim told me the truth about his summer and fall of lung cancer – his initial misdiagnosis, biopsies, scans, and slow-responding doctors, of the plan to saw his ribs off to get to his lung, his uncertainty about the choices – I offered to search for a better option. He welcomed my help. I squeezed time into late-night hours to sort through a muddle of online information. I gave him stacks of printouts to read, including the biography of a surgeon at a teaching and research hospital in Indianapolis who had an impressive track record in cancer cures.

This was the moment when our prized independence from each other began to lose its substance and grow thinner. His confession and invitation to help. My participation. But I had thought I was just a researcher, an options offerer, a short shoulder to lean on. It took only a few days in the hospital to learn how naive I was and for me to taste the bitter first inklings of what was to come.

Last month we'd left at four in morning moonlight to make the five-thirty surgery appointment at the massive hospital complex in downtown Indianapolis. Using maps I had printed out from the Internet, Jim and I found the dingy, dimly lit parking garage and tentatively walked the hospital's maze of hallways. We stood in front of a directional sign like lost children in the woods. This route would soon be as familiar to me as the path that led around the potting shed to the vegetable garden.

The pressing surgical routine would become commonplace too: Filling out stacks of forms. Then in a tiny pre-op room, sitting in the plastic chair, knees and feet together, with Jim's jeans and flannel shirt folded in a plastic hospital bag, his big, size-fourteen black sneakers on top. Jim sitting on the padded gurney in a patterned light-blue hospital gown, shoulders hunched tight with uncertainty, brows gathered. Making small talk as doctors and nurses popped in and out to ask questions and look at monitors.

When they asked who I was, I answered, *His wife.*

* * *

Hours passed while I sat in a nook of the waiting room, unread book in my lap. Thinking not about Jim or me, but about the twelve million gallons of herbicide sprayed in Vietnam, Laos, and Cambodia during the war. About the tucked-away old Polaroid Jim has of himself, a young and pink-cheeked man – more Boy Scout than marine – perched on a sandbag bunker at the horrendous Khe Sanh battle site, cigarette in hand, and, I now imagined, coated with a fine mist of trichlorophenoxyacetic acid and dioxin.

"The jungle was green when I got there and barren brown when I left," Jim had said when I'd asked him if he'd been exposed. The toxic brew showed up years later in Jim as peripheral neuropathy, non-Hodgkins lymphoma, prostate cancer, and lung cancer. Skin cancer.

Neurologic dysfunction. Headache, insomnia, and fatigue. Oh, and maybe depression and posttraumatic stress.

The cardiothoracic surgeon broke the siege of my dreary thoughts when he sat down next to me. "He's fine and in recovery," he said, knitting his dark eyebrows together under his blue bouffant sterile cap. "We were able to get the lung out without removing his ribs, but it was more difficult than expected. I had to peel his lung off of his heart where it was scarred from the non-Hodgkin's lymphoma radiation treatment," he said, his voice tight with tiredness.

Jim had hidden his lymphoma from me for twenty years, confessing it to me at the same time he told me about his lung cancer. "They said I was a dead man," he told me, explaining how he hadn't told anyone – how he didn't want it to be a topic of conversation, how amused he was that no one guessed he was sick.

I remembered what a low point it had been between us during that time, when that something that had always linked us had weakened almost to breaking. Kept in the dark, I had been ignorant of what was really going on and had drawn harsh conclusions that he let go unprotested. Jim had been lethargic and churlish, which I mistook for drunken potheadedness. In reality, he had been hiding the side effects of massive radiation treatments over the entire upper half of his body. He didn't die as forecast, and the link between us slowly strengthened again, me never knowing until so much later and then conflicted in the knowledge. Injured that he had spurned me so long ago, stunned that he had not spurned me again this round.

I slipped into a computer booth beyond the huge, oversize aquarium where brightly colored tropical fish seemed to pace like waiting family and friends. I needed to check my work email before going up to find Jim in the surgical ICU, and I wanted to look up the category the surgeon had given Jim's lung cancer.

I flipped open the medical journal I had started, a spiral notebook with dates of procedures, lists of Jim's questions, and addresses of good websites about cancer. Carefully, I keyed in the strange words stage IIA non-small cell carcinoma and quickly scrolled down the pages of information until I found what I was looking for – "five-year survival rate: 17 percent." Nothing about the drop-dead rate of the other 83 percent. I wrote it down slowly in the journal. I knew Jim would think he would be one of the 17 percent. He'd been called a dead man before.

Behind the etched-glass doors of the surgical ICU, Jim didn't look like a candidate for the 17 percent. He was shockingly shrunken and waxen. I sat at his bedside, reminding him to huff cough and to make the red spirometer ball rise under the plume of his breath in the little plastic tube, a postsurgical trick to get the lungs going again.

As the afternoon wore into evening and evening into night, heavy concern began to condense like a fog bank gathering in a valley. "His oxygen saturation levels are dropping and we don't know why," a nurse told me. Each time he fell asleep, he would startle awake from the lack of breath.

Around four or five in the morning, a worried crowd was slowly growing in his room. The jangling monitor alarms refused to be silenced. A whispered urgency rippled through the air, and I was ushered from the room. People were sleeping everywhere. Every bench, couch, and chair held a lumpy body. I found an empty bench far down the hallway. More than twenty-four hours had lumbered by since our moonlight drive to surgery. My heavy head nodded, and I curled into a semiconscious ball, huddled cold in the constricting tang of institutionalized air.

After a couple fitful hours, I woke, afraid that Jim had died while I slept. After checking his room, still full of milling medical jackets, I washed my face, smoothed my clothes, and found a nasty cup of black waiting-room coffee. I cracked the door of his room and crept invisibly into the back just in time for the seven o'clock change-of-shift nursing report.

Jim was sitting up, his hospital bed mattress cranked forward, peering over the top of an oxygen mask. With the look of a tail-tucked scared dog, his wide eyes followed me. I stood eavesdropping on the periphery, standing mutely by the windows and scratching down notes. "If he doesn't improve, we'll have to intubate him," explained one of the nurses surrounding his bed. "A specialist from respiratory therapy is on the way right now." As she spoke, a bulky, confident man in blue scrubs strode into Jim's room.

The group opened to make way.

"I hear we have a problem with oxygen saturation," he said in a lyrical East Indian intonation. He looked at the monitor. "Yes, I see, fluctuating." He ran thick, experienced hands over the equipment like a doctor palpates the bony landmarks of the spine.

"Here's the problem," he said, raising his bushy eyebrows high and holding up a piece of tubing. "This is leaking."

In a few hours I followed a well-oxygen-saturated Jim on yet another gurney to the thoracic inpatient unit several floors down, wary but sure that the situation was on the upswing. He was wheeled into a tiny, utilitarian, two-bed room that was as different from the palatial ICU as a jail cell. The neighboring bed was promisingly empty. I put Jim's belongings in one of the twin metal lockers and slumped into the plastic chrome-leg visitor chair at the end of his bed. Outside the window was a sea of gray, flat rooftops under a thick, leaden sky.

I was sure that Jim would fall right to sleep after his long, difficult night. But I was wrong. Instead his hands roamed, scratching over his body, and his restlessness grew like a virus. "My skin is so prickly," he snarled. Taking me by surprise, he threw his legs over the side of the bed and started pulling at his tubes. "Home. I'm going home. So I can get some sleep."

I jumped to quickly pull my chair into the small space by his bed to block his escape and stood next to him. "Stop, Jim," I said forcefully, looking directly into his desperate eyes. "You can't leave yet." Like the ventilator tech in ICU, I moved my hands smoothly over him, familiar with the landscape of his body, until he calmed and sat. I rotated his legs back onto the bed and pulled the sheet over him.

"I hate this damned oxygen thing; it won't stay in my nose and it itches," Jim whined.

I sat on the edge of his bed and said in my best gentle voice, "Here, let me fix that." I realigned the latex tubing over his ears, slid the adjustment ring under his chin so that it fit snugly but not too tight, and checked how the prongs sat in his nose, where the skin looked irritated. I smeared a dab of hospital hand lotion at the base of his nostrils. "There, is that better?"

He snaked a hand over to mine. It felt good to nestle his big hand inside my comparatively small hands, as if I could protect him and make everything better.

"How about something to eat?" I asked. "You aren't on a restricted diet." I picked up a restaurant-style menu that was sitting on the minuscule table between his bed and the wall. "We can order in."

"A hamburger," said Jim with a slight uptick of enthusiasm. "I want a hamburger and fries. Order something for yourself. We can eat together. It'll be like a Saturday night date."

I thought this was a good sign. He'd be napping soon, and after that we would be checking things off of his to-go-home list: eat, pee, walk, have a bowel movement, get off the oxygen. All I had to do was stay in control, distract him from itching. But as the day grew longer, I knew it wouldn't be that simple. He'd nap for about ten seconds and then wake with a start, look around wildly, complain about itching, and ask some crazy question. *Why are we waiting? Why do they page my doctor all the time – don't you hear that? Why am I here? Who are these people?* Then he would fall asleep again.

Unsure what to do, and weary, I pressed the call button for the nurse.

"It's normal for you to feel itchy and disoriented," assured his nurse, turning the pages of his chart. "It's a reaction to the morphine. Your face is flushed too," she said, noting the unusual pink in his cheeks.

"What about something to help him stay asleep?" I asked, feeling a headache coming on. "He hasn't slept well since surgery. This morning the nurse asked the doctor to prescribe a strong sleeping pill."

"It hasn't been ordered yet. I'm sure it will be." Her forearm brushed against mine as she turned to replace his chart in the door, transferring a comforting warmth. "We'll get some Benadryl for the itching. It will make you drowsy too." She smiled a wholesome, nursey smile at Jim. He smiled back.

The nurse set about making everything right in his room. She replaced a depleted IV bag with another one plump with clear fluid. She checked the ruddy-colored urine level in the bag hanging off the metal rails of the bed and marked down a number on Jim's chart in straight, even handwriting, as if there were an unseen ruler line beneath her pen. She checked his temperature. She had a precise, competent air about her. Her hair was pulled back off her face, and she wore a simple gold band wedding ring. She carried her stethoscope draped over her neck in a way that suggested years of practice. I could sense that the pockets of her white jacket were carefully stocked, and I wondered what she carried.

"You should go home and get some rest yourself," she said to me. "Come back in the morning."

There was an aching pain at my temples and in the back of my neck. I looked at the hard, blue plastic chair I would have to sleep in if I stayed. I didn't want to leave Jim alone.

"Go," said the nurse as she patted me on the back, sensing my reluctance. "We'll take good care of him, and you'll do better tomorrow with a good night's sleep."

"I'll just be sleeping," said Jim. "Go home."

I puffed out a sigh. "Okay, but you be good."

On a piece of paper torn from my notebook, I wrote instructions for Jim with my cell phone number and read them aloud to him before setting the note on the tiny table next to his bed in case he forgot where he was while I was gone:

#1 You are my sweetie.
#2 You are in the hospital recovering from lung surgery.
#3 Don't get up! You have tubes connected.
#4 I'll be back in the morning at 7:00 am.

XOXO Claire

P.S. These people are your friends.

"Go to sleep," I told him sternly. "I'll see you in the morning."

I drove the seventy-five miles home like a zombie. When I pulled into the drive, Lila and Diggity were barking like maniacs, in case I didn't know that things were amok. I let "the girls" into the house and sat on the floor with them, one arm around each dog until we all were breathing regularly. After feeding the poor, ravenous things, I stepped under the shower until the warm water turned cold, letting the anxiety wash out of me.

I got up at five, put the dogs out, and repacked my bag to take to the hospital – water, chocolate, a banana, magazines, my favorite hand lotion, a couple of books, and the spiral medical journal – and threw myself back onto the road with a cup of coffee. I knew how to do this; I was a pro. I commuted to Indianapolis for work. I slid in some good travel music, a Cyndi Lauper CD, and was soon on the highway to Jim singing along and pushing the back button to hear the song over and over.

If you're lost you can look and you will find me
Time after time
If you fall I will catch you I'll be waiting
Time after time

When I walked into Jim's hospital room, he was sitting scrunched in the corner of his bed.

"Come in, come here," Jim said in hushed, conspiratorial tones. "Where have you been? A guy stole my clothes."

"What? What happened?"

"After you left, I got a roommate," he said, waving at the empty bed just a few feet away from his. "He was a whack-case. He tore his phone out and was shouting. So I turned my back to him and decided to try to sleep. Then I woke up with him standing right here by the wall, next to my bed. I told him to get the fuck away. He said to me that he just wanted to use the phone or maybe he should beat the shit outta me."

Jim laughed, a high-pitched raving laugh. "Then I said I guess he'd just have to beat the shit outta me, because I was in no shape to fight. He didn't hit me, though. The nurse came. They wheeled him out later, in restraints. Said he'd taken a bunch of pills. But he took my clothes with him. Go look!" He pointed to one of the gray metal lockers.

The steel latch slid up easily when I opened the door to where I had stashed Jim's clothes and shoes. His shoes were there, but no bag of clothes. I opened the other door. It was empty. Maybe this theft really had happened. Good thing I had his wallet in my bag.

"But they don't believe me; they think I'm insane. They think it's my fault, that I started a fight," Jim continued frantically.

"I'm going to go talk to the nurse," I said, kissing Jim on the cheek and sure that the nurse of last night never would have let this happen. "Calm yourself. Don't go anywhere."

The nurses' station was far away from Jim's corner room, and I hurriedly walked the corridor, not wanting to leave Jim for another second. No one was at the station. Four office chairs, stacks of paperwork, blinking phones. I looked around, feeling as if I were in a discount store with no hope of finding anyone who could tell me where to find the soap.

I scurried back to Jim's room and pushed the call button for the nurse. After what seemed like eons, a round-faced nurse I had never seen came into the room.

"Yes, there was a problem overnight with his roommate," she said when I asked.

"This is no good," I said. "Jim is upset, and his clothes are gone."

"His clothes are gone?" said the puzzled nurse.

"Yes. Look. His locker is empty, except for his shoes," I said, opening the door for her.

"He had clothes in here?" asked the skeptical nurse.

"Yes. In the bag we brought with us from ICU. He didn't come to the hospital in a patient gown," I said, exasperated.

"You didn't take them home?"

I could feel her suspicion that Jim and I were both nuts, and wrath boiled up out of the knot in my stomach.

"Has he slept?" I asked. "Did he get the sleep meds?"

"No, he's not sleeping, and they're afraid that the sleep medications will only make it worse," said the nurse as she turned to leave. "The morphine is causing his restlessness and paranoia. And the Benadryl gives him insomnia instead of making him drowsy."

I felt my dander rise further, and I started giving instructions.

"Call the doctor," I said in a not-to-be-denied voice. "I want him in a private room. And I want help with him when I can't be here. Surely he isn't the first to have these problems. And I want someone to find his clothes," I continued with authority. "Now. This is ridiculous and completely unacceptable."

The nurse nodded her head and began edging down the hallway away from me. "I'll see what I can do," she said noncommittally.

* * *

It took all day and all the next day of me being a bitch, but Jim got his private room. He also got an overnight volunteer whose job it was to tell him where he was and what was going on and to alert the nurses if things got out of hand. His medications were straightened out, and he slept. His clothes, which the other man had actually worn, were returned laundered. He was soon released, with little to show for the trauma but a glaring red lateral thoracotomy scar. But something had fundamentally shifted between us.

We had violated the space between us. I had made decisions about his life without asking him; he, ever strong, had shown me his white belly of vulnerability. A new unbidden intimacy was twining between us, searching for all of our secret nooks and crannies.

3

Waterloo

By the February following Jim's surgery and his move into the house, we were in our regular places at the oncologist's office at the hospital. Jim was sitting upright on the exam table. I was in the little plastic chair, jotting down notes and making sure we covered everything on the Questions for the Doctor list. Jim looked like a concentration camp prisoner – bald, sunken eyes, cheekbones prominent – and I felt like one, after a long, clamped-down chemotherapy winter.

The doctor sat on his examining stool across from us. I took comfort in the smoothness of his creamy coffee complexion and poised manner, the flawless crispness of his white lab coat. He was listening carefully as Jim recited his problems – chills, fatigue, memory loss, diarrhea, confusion.

"These things will linger and then mostly fade after this last chemo treatment," the doctor said confidently. "We will follow you, take images, and hope your lungs are still clear in six months. In the meantime, enjoy your life, don't start smoking again, and eat a healthy diet. If this comes back, it likely will kill you." My gut contracted as the 17 percent dice rolled invisibly in the small room.

The doctor paused and placed Jim's file on the cabinet. He looked at Jim squarely and spoke slowly. "We humans have it backward. We take life for granted and treat death as if it's only a possibility. But death is for certain, so focus on life."

On the way home, I almost said how cool it was for the doctor to say that. I glanced over at Jim. His pale face was sagging from the exertion of the day.

Before I had a chance to stick my foot in my mouth, Jim spoke. "What a jerk that doctor is," he snarled. "Easy for him to say, 'focus on life.' I bet he says that to all his patients. It's his pat line. I'm not taken in. He thinks I'm a goner. I didn't go through all of this to die; I'm beating this."

He had a good point. It's much easier to feel good about dying if it's not you. That poor doctor who sees glum cancer patients hour after hour, day after day – it probably *was* his pat line. What else could he say?

But Jim wasn't the average cancer patient. Before he'd been diagnosed with lung cancer, he was already a member of the unlikely survival club. Jim had lived through Vietnam when his marine buddies were killed. While working in Alaska he'd survived and recovered from a terrible accident that had ripped off his ear and stolen his short-term memory for months. His non-Hodgkin's, skin, and prostate cancers had scarred but not claimed him. Seventeen percent survival seemed doable. All he had to do was get to the end of summer with his lungs clear.

*   *   *

On a stifling, humid August day, Jim drove by himself to the six-months-post-chemo appointment. "Let's not make it a big deal," he said superstitiously before he left. "Then maybe it won't be a big deal. I'll go without you as if it were a regular checkup, as if everything were normal, so it will be."

I was on pins and needles all day. I knew he wouldn't call. Whatever the news, he would deliver it in person. I zoomed home early from work. The pole barn doors were open. I rushed from the truck to hear the no-big-deal news.

Inside the workshop, Jim looked up from the custom gear mechanism he was building. A broad smile broke across the horizon of his face. "My lungs are still clear. The oncologist called me a survivor."

"Survivor," I said slowly, turning over the word over in my mouth like a smooth, sweet piece of hard candy – trying not to notice the sour taste along its edges. Did "survivor" mean a survivor who lives to die of something else, or did it mean survivor as in *17 percent survived five years*? But I pushed the bitter thought aside. Jim was ecstatic. He was focusing on life, and I was jumping on board.

"Let's celebrate," said Jim, putting down his tools. "I bought two thick steaks on the way home. Heat up the grill, drink wine, and plan a vacation to take yet this year." A magical elfishness was in the air around him as he walked across the room to kiss me.

Night overcame us and cooled as we sat on the back patio feeding steak scraps to the dogs, who sat in well-behaved attention next to us. The wine bottle was empty. Beyond the vegetable garden, fireflies sparkled and retreated to the trees while the summer cicadas throbbed. We'd decided on Nova Scotia. We'd never been to the northeast and Nova Scotia was as far northeast as we could get in the truck. As a bonus we could drive back home by way of Pennsylvania to hunt for Jim's Irish immigrant ancestors.

*   *   *

But in mid-September Jim unwillingly left the 17 percent. We had made the trip and had just finished big, satisfying bowls of fish chowder crammed with clams, scallops, and hunks of cod, haddock, halibut, and pollack at the White Gull restaurant in Lockeport on Nova Scotia's Atlantic side. We were lazily walking back to our B&B

beside the bay, captivated by an idyllic sunset of gold ribbons mirrored in the tranquil water of the harbor. By a pile of sharp boulders we stopped to watch the reflecting colors sink into umber and red.

Suddenly Jim was down. He had fallen forward onto the nearby rock pile and jammed his foot in crooked between the chunks of granite.

I steadied him into a seated position and pulled his foot out.

"My ankle," said Jim, massaging his leg. "I think I sprained it."

"What happened?" I asked. I scooted over to sit beside him on the uncomfortable rocks.

"I dunno. It was like my legs gave out. One minute I'm standing, the next I've fallen." Jim pulled the leg of his jeans past his muscular calf and worked his foot back and forth. "But it doesn't mean anything. I'm sixty-one; I'm starting to get old, that's all."

Ignored little incidents of increased unsteadiness and a worrisome re-fogging of his thoughts had been traveling along with us for the whole trip. It was as if the effects of chemo were returning, but not quite the same. I didn't know what to say to him. Jim didn't want to give voice or power to the idea that something was seriously wrong. But I could hear the scythe beginning to swing in the distance.

The next day, we caught the last ferry of the season back to Maine, and the following morning we started the diagonal drive home by way of Pennsylvania to find the grave of his ancestor. Jim had a headache that wouldn't go away, so I did all the driving through hours of thick thunderstorms, peering through the windshield bisected by the blue *V* of the straps that held our canoe tight to the front of the truck. Jim slumped in the corner of the passenger seat, his face and lips loose. The dogs, who had frolicked along the waters of Digby Neck and swum in crystal-clear Kejimkujik Lake, napped in curled balls in the camper shell, occasionally waking to thrust their wet noses through the pass-through window to sniff the breeze for whatever was next.

A curving two-lane highway glistened black when the late-afternoon sun broke through the clouds. White farmhouses with wraparound covered porches and peaked dormer windows lined the road that followed a broad mountain valley. Black horses drawing Amish carriages, some open and some enclosed, briskly trotted on the road.

I roused Jim. "Look. Look how pretty."

He rubbed his temples and squinted. Scooting up in the seat and looking around, he said, "We'll never find the cemetery."

"Yes, we will. I printed out the map from the Internet. In fact, I think it's just ahead." At the bend of the road, by a well-kept, single-story brick church with a white gingerbread steeple, was the town of Waterloo and the Upper Tuscarora Cemetery. We walked for a long time, braiding our way through tombstones, before we found Jim's immigrant forefather. I left Jim standing pensively at the tall white marker, his chin in his hand. I sat in the truck with the passenger door open, the dogs watching him among the graves until the sun began to move toward the mountain-ridge horizon.

I wondered what he was thinking and why he was staying so long. Was he imagining the trip from Ireland across the ocean to Pennsylvania? Was he aligning Irish history with the dates on the gravestone? Was he thinking about the fights between the settlers and the Indians? Was he considering his own mortality?

A low mountain mist was gathering by the time he leisurely walked back to us. He leaned on the open door with a puzzled look on his face.

"I can't remember how the family lineage goes," he said.

Suddenly I understood. He'd been standing there the whole time trying to remember what he'd repeated to me hundreds of times over the years. So often, in fact, that I had it memorized myself. Hoping I had hidden my shock, I slowly recited the male generations for him. He nodded his head and scooted me over to the driver's seat, the 17 percent hanging in silent jeopardy.

Then Jim smiled and broke into song. *"Waterlooooo. Waterlooooo. Where will you meet your Waterloo? Every puppy has his day; everybody has to pay; everybody has to meet his Waterloo."* Turning around to the dogs, he bayed, and we all joined in. *"Waterloooooooo."*

* * *

A week later I was tired of arguing with Jim over what was happening.

Since we'd gotten home from vacation, his memory was all wrong. I had to help him balance his checkbook. He was misspelling words by adding extra letters, as if every word were *Mississippi.* He couldn't remember what he read. His handwriting was deteriorating. Added to that were dizziness, headaches, and bumblefootedness. He insisted it was a worsening of his low blood pressure, and he obstinately made an appointment with his family doctor for more than a week away. Fury from his playing so loosely with his symptoms while time ticked by gathered like a hard ball in my chest.

Without asking, I called Jim's doctor and tried to play my wife card. "Please, could you move up his appointment? I'm worried about him," I begged the nurse.

"I can't talk to you about his care," she said haughtily. "That's against patient privacy. If he wants, he can call the doctor. If it's an emergency, he should go to the ER."

I decided to try to get Jim to call his doctor.

"You did what?" said Jim angrily when I told him what I had done. "You have overstepped your bounds."

I knew he was trying to put things back to normal and reestablish our customary boundaries, because that would make everything okay. But I also knew everything wasn't okay.

"I'm the only one who is looking at this realistically," I argued. "Don't screw around. Stop downplaying your symptoms. This is serious."

"I can tell whether or not I'm having an emergency," Jim said pointedly as he sat on the kitchen stool to steady himself. "I don't need to call, because it isn't serious. It can't be serious, because it comes and goes."

"Read this paragraph, then, and tell me what it says." I shoved a magazine in his direction.

He read it out loud and accurately summarized what it said.

"Add this." I scribbled down a column of hard numbers on the back of a nearby envelope and handed him a pencil.

He added them perfectly.

"See, I'm fine," he said hotly. "Don't worry. And butt out." He got up and stalked away to his downstairs living space. The red stoplight between our floors was definitely on.

Jim was more circumspect the next morning at breakfast. "I didn't feel so good last night. I couldn't keep my balance. My legs were weak. My head hurt all night. I couldn't see well."

"Let's make a list," I said as if yesterday's conversation had not happened. I turned to a clean page in the medical notebook, and wrote List of Complaints. "There's the watery-swirly vision, headaches, weak legs, and dizziness that you had on vacation. And there's the new stuff – not getting words right, remembering, adding and subtracting, forming letters. What have I missed?"

"You should note that it comes and goes," he said. "There's also bloating, gut pain, and bowel changes. But I think that's because you made me eat all that fish in Nova Scotia." Jim yawned and scooted back from the counter. "I'm still sleepy. I think I'll go take a nap."

He disappeared to the lower level of the house and didn't come back. Early in the evening, I heard the downstairs television turn on.

I joined him, bringing him a cup of coffee. "How are you feeling? Are you hungry?"

"Still tired, but not hungry." He shifted in his chair and held his coffee with two hands. "Let's do something besides talk about my problems. Let's watch a movie. *Troy* has just started."

I settled into the couch and the hope that our Saturday night would be just a regular Saturday night.

When Achilles slew a giant warrior with one dorky blow in front of obviously computer-generated armies, I turned toward Jim to complain. But because of the look on his face, I didn't speak. It was so odd. A cloudy, foreign vagueness.

Jim put his head in his hands. "I've had some kind of event. Something in my brain. It's like I'm super-stoned. We should go to the ER, right now." He stood unsteadily.

*   *   *

Jim and I were soon back in our regular places in the narrow hospital exam room. He was sitting on the ER gurney, and I was in an orange plastic chair, pen poised to take notes. Jim's face was a grim green in the pale fluorescent light.

A young doctor stood near the door. He cleared his throat and looked uncertain about where to look. "The CT scan revealed brain tumors."

Jim and I looked at each other, our eyes locked at the unwanted news.

An illogical guilt ran down my skin like a cold chill. My knowing that something was wrong had proved to be right. Maybe if I hadn't made a big deal of it, the doctor would have said it was low blood pressure, and just as the oncologist had told him last summer, he was a survivor.

* * *

Two and a half weeks later, as the daylight grew shorter in early October, a surgeon made a little hinged door on the back of Jim's skull and scooped out three tumors. This time after surgery Jim went to the spartan neurosurgical ICU. His single room was as small as a closet.

His eyes fluttered open when I walked in. I tried to avoid looking at the terrifying bandages wrapped around his head. I placed a small glass vase holding two vibrant orange gerbera daisies tucked into a dark green fern on his tray table, the only flat surface in the tiny room.

"This is you and me walking in the woods on a fall day under a bright blue sky," I said, the best good excuse I could come up with for bringing flowers.

He smiled wanly and said, "I'm very itchy."

I set down my expertly packed hospital bag (water, magazines, chocolate, a pillow, hand lotion) and pressed the call button for the nurse. The straight-backed visitor chair didn't look like a comfortable place to spend the night, but I wasn't going to let him be alone.

* * *

When Jim got home he was immediately better. He balanced his checkbook and used his table saw. But his percentage had dropped.

Two years. That's what the neurosurgeon told Jim before he left the hospital. "If you have whole brain radiation, you'll likely survive two years. Without it, the tumors will be back for certain. It has to be done within three weeks."

Whole brain radiation – zapping the entire brain with several rounds of radiation to kill any remaining cancer cells – is a detonating phrase no one wants to hear. It got worse when I looked it up online: progressive and permanent damage, decreased intellect and memory, increased confusion, or full-blown dementia. What kind of two-year survivorship was that? A pros-and-cons conversation about the treatment followed us around for days from kitchen to patio to bedroom to living room.

"I don't want to do it, but I'm doing it," Jim decided. "There's still a percentage, a chance I could beat it. Once you're dead, you're dead. There's no coming back or changing your mind."

I felt a failing in my response, as if I couldn't draw upon the nutrients I needed in order to take this next step. It was like I needed an extra boost, a top dressing of compost, to get me through a hard season. But there was no gardener to care for me.

Even though I had looked up and printed out and read aloud everything I could find about the malevolent, sort-of-life-saving whole brain radiation, I could hardly hold an opinion about it. I no longer had insight or feelings. I was adrift and spacey, as if I were suffering brain damage myself.

"You know, you don't have to do this too," Jim said to me, noticing my drooping interaction. "You don't have brain cancer." In a twisted way I did share Jim's brain cancer, like a man who empathetically shares pregnancy with his wife.

Then, like an evil cancer ghost, Jim's non-Hodgkin's radiation of years past slowed the urgent treatment – one week, two weeks, three weeks. If the new radiation overlapped where the old doses fell, there would be permanent open sores. His ancient medical file was ambiguous about where the old doses had stopped at the base of his skull. Calculation after calculation was made, the doctors agreeing that guessing was better than nothing. Twenty radiation blasts to the head spanning two weeks around a sure-to-be-bleak Thanksgiving holiday were planned and begun.

Three days into the blasting, Jim was surprised when he poured his hot morning coffee not into his cup, but onto the counter instead.

But it was the intense headache behind Jim's left eye that made the doctors interrupt the treatments for new brain scans. The masses had come back, and they were all over his brain. I felt the ground beneath our feet grow steep and slippery.

Broad-spectrum whole brain radiation was scrapped for something that sounded even scarier – *fractionated stereotactic radiosurgery*. It would zero in on the determined tumors. After lots more scans and tests, they would zap Jim's brain four times over four late December days.

It took all of my flagging energy to be with him, but I couldn't sleep for an incessant, empty buzz that ran through my body. I stayed up late playing Space Cadet 3D pinball on the computer, causing Jim to complain of strange pinging noises in his dreams. Going to work was nearly unbearable; I wanted to take family leave, but didn't. I couldn't afford months without pay. I had to wait to see what would happen. Jim's busy appointment schedule was tough for me, and one day I couldn't get out of work for an appointment. So we asked his sister to take him. It was a mistake.

She had been pushing a vegetarian, no-cancer diet and an array of supplements that Jim rejected. Wounding her, he always threw away the bottles of expensive pills and powders that she brought over and dumped the food she made for him, nasty-tasting concoctions with who-knows-what in them. As emotional as Jim was not, she was. Quick-tempered, but also just as bright and sure of herself as he was. Arguments flared regularly between them. She didn't do well in medical settings, spun out emotionally when things got tough.

But we had to ask someone for help, and we asked her to take him to a CT scan. Seemed like it would be simple. She could drive him to Indianapolis and back.

That evening I came home from work to find Jim and his sister sitting downstairs. I collapsed, tired, in the corner chair, kicked my shoes off, and realized I had walked in on a quarrel. From his lounger Jim was looking drawn and remote – he'd hardly acknowledged my arrival. His sister, thin and jumpy, was perched tensely on the couch near him.

She briefly glared at me before turning back to Jim. "Why won't you listen? I've told you for months how to build up your immune system to fight the cancer. Why do you keep eating meat and sugar?" She reached into her backpack and pulled out a packet of brochures. She thrust them into Jim's hands.

I recognized them; they were from that out-of-state cancer hospital with TV ads that almost guarantee recovery.

"At least do this," she said pleadingly. "I called these people and told them about you. They recommend different treatments than the ones you are getting and want you to come. They cure cancer. Go, and give them a try."

"I don't want to die in Tulsa," Jim shot back in a weary voice. "Those religious, nut-case quacks are in it just for the money. And I don't believe all that wheat-grass-smoothie malarkey."

"You're doing everything wrong. You're listening to the establishment because of *her*." She'd jabbed a crooked arthritic finger my direction, swiveling to glower at me.

"This is your fault. You've influenced him. You believe in the system. You, you, *you*," she sputtered, "are a passive dumbbell. I curse you now and forever. Once he croaks, I will never have anything to do with you again."

She lurched up the stairs and slammed out the door.

In the silence she left behind, I wanted to laugh at her wimpy *dumbbell* insult. Couldn't she come up with something better than that? *Shit-for-brains* maybe.

Then Jim told me how she'd melted down while driving home from the appointment – shouting, speeding, running over curbs, taking wrong turns, and getting lost. "She always has to make everything about her," he said bitterly. "It's because she was sick as a little girl and doted upon, catered to. She doesn't know how to deal with life. I worry most about her. What will she do if I die? Who will look out for her?"

Indeed. It was her grief that had exploded. I think it was the shock, the clarity of his certain death, that blew the cap off her fury and fear. She'd only seen the sick Jim in his living room, a controlled setting where he stayed in his chair. She hadn't seen him stumbling and confused in the larger world.

I was habituated to the sick Jim, but I wasn't prepared for what rapidly came next. There was no improvement. Jim's headache persisted and he still couldn't find the cup for his coffee. I watched morbidly riveted as new symptoms coiled around him.

He forgot how to work the ATM machine. He drifted eerily to the right when he walked. He had a stumbling gait. His hands trembled.

"The fog comes on little cat feet," said Jim, his wryness still intact. "But it builds up. I can't recognize myself in the mirror anymore." The man who had been so handsome was a ghoul of his former self. Except for a small monk's ring low on the back of his head, his hair was permanently gone from the radiation. Always lean, he was now bloated from steroids, with a huge gut and a ravenous, chemically induced appetite – the opposite of the typical scrawny cancer patient.

Then, one morning as he slid onto the stool for breakfast, Jim said, "My vision is doubled. But only when I cover one eye." Horror must have spread across my face when I looked at him. How do you tell someone that his eyes are crossed? I can't remember how I did it. What I remember was feeling that we were sliding faster and faster down a demonized Dante's circle of cancer hell.

Jim banned Lila and Diggity from the house, afraid they would knock him over and finding their smell unbearable. They lived almost feral, slept in a straw-stuffed doghouse on a half acre that we had fenced in and gleefully named Dog Paradise back in brighter days, and held vigil at the back door in hopes of a reprieve.

He banned all friends from the house. No one could see him like this.

In late January, almost a year after Jim's brain surgery, new scrolling digital MRI images showed tumor masses blossoming on the computer screen with the velocity of a tornado sweeping across the countryside. Jim was fitted for a mesh mask to hold his head immobile, and a new series of amped-up, high-dose radiation treatments were started but then suspended when he convulsed during a session.

I sat numbly through my first ever poor annual work performance review, waiting for my boss to finish so that I could request family leave. At the end of the recital of my failures, I could barely rally up the energy to respond. "Whatever," I actually said before turning in the family leave papers. I wished I had done it months ago, that I could go back and reclaim the days I had given to work and give them to Jim instead. Good thing we were married, or I wouldn't have been able to get the unpaid leave.

We knew what the answer would be when we went in for the last three-hour round of MRIs, but we went anyway, just in case. Cancer had escaped to the lining of Jim's brain and shot down his spinal fluid to circulate everywhere. I shook my head at the inappropriate language of cancer. When I first heard that the scans had shown "enhancements," I'd thought it was a good thing.

"You may last a month," the neurosurgeon said. "You may only make it two days. But here's an experimental drug to try."

Jim and I stared wordlessly at the prescription in my quivering hand, a last minuscule percentage. But it wouldn't be Jim's. His percentage would be zero in just ten days.

4

Terminal Restlessness

It was a bland, colorless February afternoon. Elvis Presley was singing *Don't Be Cruel* from a collection of CDs we'd ordered from an infomercial on a long-ago Saturday night.

We were having fun, singing along, almost forgetting that Jim was dying, when suddenly he couldn't breathe. Open-mouth panting, panicky crossed eyes. His inhalations rattled. I quickly turned on the floor fan as hospice had suggested and kneeled next to his chair, taking his hand in mine to get his attention.

"Breathe with me. Inhale through your nose. Wait. Then exhale through your mouth." After all these months he still couldn't remember to do this; he still needed me to show him, to do it with him. It only took a few rounds for his eyes to stop rolling and his alarm to melt away.

It was up to me to keep everything on an even keel. I did it by being in do-mode. Do this, do that. Do-mode was the only place left for me. I was fueled by the buzzing that now penetrated to my cellular level like an endless caffeine high.

"I'm sick of that old pop music," Jim said harshly. "Take it off. Find something else to play. Something smooth."

"How about *Circular Breathing*, that tribal didgeridoo stuff?" I plucked a CD from his bookshelf and held it up for him to see.

Jim laughed, getting my lamebrain joke. "Sure. Maybe it will help."

A primal bass droning filled the lower level of the house. As I turned to sit on the couch across from Jim, the phone rang, jangling me up again.

It was Jim's sister. Hearing her voice surprised me, because she had quit talking to us since the CT appointment incident. Three stubborn months had passed mutely in a sibling standoff. Jim wouldn't call her. She wouldn't call him.

Sure that he would die before she gave in, he'd written a letter to her last week and asked me to read it, to check for errors.

I remember it as being lighthearted in a big-brotherly way, a final note to her about knowing that happiness was possible if you looked for it. He'd written that he knew because he had just recently found it. I'd wondered if it wasn't really my assistance with spelling that he wanted, but to let me know how he felt in a roundabout way. A pretty radical thing for a guy who never talked about his feelings.

"Mail this the day I die," Jim had instructed me. "And promise that you will be nice to my sister after I am dead. She's going to need friends. She'll be the last one of my family alive."

In our final months together, we shared a strange peace. A horrific contentment in the vortex of disaster and fear, like the calm in the center of a swirling tornado. In response, our connection had thickened into a cable of charged light alive between us.

Jim was making me promise all kinds of things. To burn his drawings and journals. To write the sparsest of obituaries. To not hold any services. This promise about his sister was a hard one.

"Okay," I'd said, thinking it would be easy to be nice to his sister if I never saw her again, as she had promised.

Now here she was on the line. I handed the phone to Jim and watched him as he yessed and noed and okayed his way through the conversation with his sister.

He handed me the phone to hang up. "She's coming over right now," he said as if nothing had happened. "She has a DVD copy of the film from our old eight-millimeter camera. Says it's wild."

When I opened the door for her, she scowled at the do-not-resuscitate notice for ambulance crews taped to the front door and gave me a perfunctory nod. I stepped back, letting her walk down the steps ahead of me into the lower level, which was humming with the deep vibrations of the still-playing didgeridoo CD.

She sank into the couch as if she had never left and waved the disc in the air. "It's very bizarre," she said to Jim. "I think you'll like it."

Like an unacknowledged servant, I took the disc, slid it into the player for them, and pushed the remote button. Hundreds of photographs flew by on the screen at an incredible pace that magically dovetailed with the didgeridoo drone. I wondered how it looked to Jim with his crossed-eyes double vision.

"It's because we used a movie camera mostly to take single shots," she said to Jim. "Each frame is a separate photo and it plays like a crazy movie. Since we used it to shoot movies too, there are stretches of short action as well."

We were riveted by the images whizzing in sync with the throbbing didgeridoo. Mildred the cat. Shawn the dog. Marti the girlfriend. Mom and her sexy, black Monte Carlo. Jim juggling. A road trip to California. Riding horses bareback across a big pasture. They were all young in a world I was never part of – it was an era before me.

Then a chilling but comic thought dawned on me: this was Jim's life literally flashing before his eyes. "I think I'll leave you to it, go catch some fresh air," I said after a bit, knowing they needed time together without me.

My feet headed for the overgrown trail in the woods behind the house. The dogs ran along on the other side of the fence, barking and hoping I would take them with me. But I needed some time away from responsibility. Lavender blackberry canes clawed my cheeks as I stumbled under low-hanging branches of leafless pawpaw trees, my stride clumsy from inactivity. Springing over a downed tree, I caught my toe and plowed facedown into icy, moldy leaves. Rubbing my scuffed hands, I sat on the log, my mind wandering, glad to be free for a while.

"Our confinement," I'd written in my journal. I knew *confinement* often referred to childbirth – the beginning of a life instead of the end of a life, but I liked it better than *deathwatch*. It was a suitable term anyway. Jim and I were lying in, confined to smaller and smaller spaces, every sliver of independence relinquished. I even slept on the floor right next to his bed so that I could hear him if he tried to get up in the night to pee – he always forgot he couldn't walk.

Jim wanted to be close to me. He was scared, not of death, but of dying.

"It's hard for me lose my brain," he'd said at the beginning of the radiation treatments. "It's my most favorite pet. Find me a fast way out in case I need it."

A big dose of gin and valium sounded perfect. We'd agreed to do it according to the directions I'd found in Derek Humphry's *Final Exit*, the euthanasia textbook. But his sister, visiting before the big fight, had found the instructions on his bookcase.

"What's this?" she'd said, flipping through the pages I had copied.

"Oh, nothing," I'd said, taking them from her. But we knew her discovery had eliminated the option. She would surely call for an autopsy (local newspaper headline: "Wife Charged with Assisted Suicide after Victim's Sister Insists on Coroner's Investigation").

Earlier this week Jim had pleaded with me. "Do I really have to go through this? Please, Claire, get my dad's .45 out of the closet. Just one bullet in the head. Give me the gun. I'll do it."

"No, I can't," I'd said, looking away in betrayal. The never-to-be-forgotten image of his crossed eyes was enough for me. But him with a bullet through the brain? Top of his head blown off from the eye sockets up? Cleaning up his splattered brain? That vision was not going to be in my future.

Awareness of my cold butt on the wet log seeped in and brought me back to reality. It was time to go back.

I quietly opened the front door, listening. The deep bass didg-eridoo was still vibrating. I jerked off my dirty boots while girding myself to greet the scene downstairs.

"Helloooo," I cheerfully called while coming down the steps. A raw truce was in the air. Jim gave me that dreamy, grateful look he'd had of late. His sister, crowlike, flapped to her feet, smiled darkly at me, and mumbled good-bye.

"Let's have soup," I chirped in her wake.

Jim had difficulty swallowing; it's a bane of the dying.

He couldn't drink coffee – it was too thin; so I made coffee pud-ding. He couldn't handle chunks – they were too thick, so I bought a muscular blender to whir food into a puree. I served it in cheerful, normal-looking, Campbell's "sippable soup" cups – one for him and one for me – to keep from pointing out his problem.

At each visit the nurses from hospice would ask if he wanted those canned chocolate and strawberry nutrition drinks. He'd shake his head politely and say, "No, I like what Claire fixes." The lack of decent food was something I could make all better, maybe the only thing left that I could control.

But going to the kitchen, leaving Jim alone, was tricky. A few days ago, when I was upstairs, he'd decided to get up from his chair solo to go pee, probably thinking he could lean against things on the way to the john. A loud thump on the hospice baby monitor made me run down the steps to find him wedged in the doorway of the bathroom, not breathing, a seizure passing.

I'd strong-armed his steroid-bloated body around so that his nose was not smashed flat on the floor. I called his name, and just when I believed he was dead, he had jerked big breaths back to life, wondering why in the hell he was jammed in the doorway. Panic had frozen me in the narrow hallway the first time it happened. Now I was used to his seizures. He'd had plenty.

I had just put the soup in the microwave when I heard the familiar thump on the monitor again. I bolted down the steps, and there he was, impossibly squeezed half in and half out of the bathroom. Not breathing. His clothes soaked in urine.

I knew the seizure pattern. Again I heaved his heavy body upright. His pushed-up shirt revealed the green and black bruises from other falls. I called his name. Again he came back, again surprised to find himself on the floor.

Pushing, shoving, and pulling together, we managed to get him up into the wheelchair and then into bed. He was bruised but not broken. He wanted to be naked, how he liked to sleep. I cleaned him and put new pads on his bed. No one cared about soup anymore.

"I'm disgusting," said Jim. "Call for a catheter." We'd been putting off getting a catheter, thinking it would be easier without it, but all day we'd been changing pads and clothes; we were both tired of it. He drifted off propped up on pillows. I sat next to him, watching him sleep until the hospice nurse came around midnight.

She put in the urinary catheter and adjusted his meds. Jim was agitated and irritable, out of breath. I scrambled to change the timing and dosages of drugs written in my medical journal, now thick with notes. Nine dizzying columns: Mouth Sores, Seizures, Edema, Air Hunger/Pain, Secretions, Anxiety, Regular Pain, Stool Softener, and Sleep.

As the nurse was gathering her bags to leave, she said, "You'll need help getting through the night. Do you have a friend to ask?"

"Sure, I guess." I was taken aback.

"Good. Be sure to call if you have questions." And then she left.

I stood still for a while trying to understand what had just happened, then busied myself gathering the piles of wet sweatpants and blankets to put in the washer. I tried to think. Why did I need help? Why hadn't I asked her what she meant? Why hadn't she stayed? Who might be the right companion to see Jim like this: pale, naked, collapsing, bald from radiation, bloated from steroids?

I started going down the short list of possibilities. My daughter was on the road traveling to Illinois. My oldest friend was in Florida. Another good friend didn't answer the phone. Who else could I surprise with this awful request at this hour? Maybe Pauline, the wife of one of Jim's friends. She was a convalescent nurse.

She answered right away and agreed immediately to pack a bag and come for the night. It was as if she expected my call. Just as I hung up the phone, relieved that I'd found someone but nervous because we weren't close friends, Jim jerked into another seizure – a scary, violent, and breathless one – but at least in his bed, not the doorway. At last he opened his eyes and took a breath. I must have looked scared, because when he figured out where he was and what had happened, he said, "Don't worry, I'll be okay."

With his last words, he comforted *me*.

Minutes after Pauline arrived, Jim began to fight. He wanted up and out, just like that day in the hospital after lung surgery, but worse. Thrashing around, arms and legs everywhere, he complained of no air. He'd been so compliant, so quiet, so polite, so utterly bored until now when the zero percent certainty yawned blackly before him.

This, I would learn later online, is a condition of the dying called terminal restlessness, also known as agitated delirium or terminal anguish. Maybe this was what the hospice nurse foresaw, what Pauline knew was coming.

He fought me, naked, his arms still strong and powerful, shoving and furious. I held him while I oddly ignored Pauline and frantically called hospice for advice on medication. With the phone jammed between my shoulder and my ear, I knelt and battled a gasping Jim on his bed.

I caught his head and turned his chin toward me. Nose to nose, eye to eye, I counted calming breaths out loud with him. The nurse's voice in my ear was telling me to up his dosage of Valium and to stop counting, that it wouldn't work. But she was wrong. I talked him down from the tormented place he had gone. Pauline put her hand on my shoulder and whispered I had done well. Jim relaxed and fell back onto his pillow. His hazel eyes hung hard on mine.

Idiot me didn't know it would be our last look, so I didn't really look back, not with my whole consciousness. I was foolishly busy listening to the nurse on the phone instead of being present in this last, precious, irreclaimable moment with him. This mistake haunts me yet today. His last look. My not seeing.

He's gone to sleep, I thought, not realizing he'd lost consciousness.

All night long Pauline and I sat next to his bed. She held up his catheter bag filled with dark urine and told me his kidneys had quit working. I blathered on to her about how I would be just fine after Jim died, that we'd been grieving together during his whole illness, that in some ways it would be a relief. Yesterday a nurse had told me that he probably had weeks yet. A hospital bed would be here tomorrow. I didn't get that this was his last night.

Just before dawn Pauline nudged me and said, "Pay attention. His respiration is slowing; he's about to go."

And he did. He stopped breathing and simply disappeared, along with our binding gold cord.

5

Buzzing

I hadn't planned what I would do in the moments after Jim's chest quit moving, in the hour before the mortuary men came to collect his body. And I didn't realize how quickly he would change from being Jim to being a corpse.

My first instinct was to get him untethered from the catheter. Lucky for me, Pauline was around to remove it. After that, I wasn't sure of the protocol. Should I put pennies on his closed eyes to keep them from springing vacantly open? Should I pull the blanket over his face? Wash him? Sing songs or read prayers to help his soul cross over?

But his eyes appeared tightly closed, and it didn't seem like Jim needed any help getting out of this world. If there is any truth to the belief of spirits departing, I think he left right after that last look I had missed before he slipped into unconsciousness. Stopping breathing was something his body did, not something he did. What was left on the bed was not him. It was a dead thing I hardly recognized with ugly, purple blood pooling under the skin on one side. While the acrid smell of his fear and urine still hung in the air, there was no rising specter, no lingering spirit. Just a void and a body. I knew that Jim would want his body to go to the cremation fire fuss-free.

I forced my exhausted self to call hospice to get all the after-death details going – body removal, no autopsy, cancel the hospital bed order. When I hung up the phone, I stood in his room feeling corpse-like myself – heavy and leaden but with that familiar nervous buzz picking up intensity. I've always had lots of energy. I'm a busy person by nature. But this anxious buzz was different. It vibrated through my sleep-deprived being like electricity plays through iron, finally arcing into an ignited urgency to rid illness and death from the house.

My eyes fastened onto Jim's big, black athletic shoes. I snatched them from the floor by his bed, clutching them to my chest, and ran with them to the garage. Tucking the shoes under my arm, I pried off the lid of the garbage container and threw them in. Slamming and locking down the lid, I clamped my hand across my mouth and held my breath. It was unbearable to know he would never put them on again. Outside, the winter morning was still, the winds yet to be aroused, but I was sure that I heard evil wraiths pushing their unruly roots deep into the frozen soil surrounding the house.

My anxiety rose. A list of awful things that had to go was spinning fast in my brain. Bottles of pills. The oxygen tank. Absorbent padding. The wheelchair. The baby monitor. All out, out, out. I yanked open the door to the house and flew down the steps. "Pauline," I shouted. "Help me get all of the hospice stuff packed up."

We had collected a big pile of awful when the dogs started to go wild with barking in the side yard. I walked up the steps and peered out the door to see Diggity slamming her front paws into the fence again and again while Lila ran back and forth, low with raised hackles, as a black hearse slowly swung into the drive.

Big-bellied men arose from both sides of the car. I held the door open while ripping the do-not-resuscitate notice off the glass. "Hush, now," I shouted uselessly to the dogs. The two mortuary men greeted me with the practiced solemnity of undertakers. I pushed down the loathing of this gruesome task as I led the procession down the stairs to Jim's stiffening body.

I was fine until I turned to see the gurney touch the steps to the lower level. That's when I heard a wail emerge from me like the shriek of a banshee. My prepared, practical self stood invisibly to one side watching a panicky me throw my arms up against the wall of Jim's living room and lean into sobbing. Everything stopped, and all eyes rotated toward me.

As quickly as it came, the wail extinguished itself. Like a tornadic rise and drop of temperature, the panicky me disappeared and the in-control me rearranged my face and straightened my shirt. "Sorry, I'm fine," I said to no one in particular. Wordlessly, everyone shifted their eyes away from me and back to the cart. Pauline, with her convalescent nursing experience, and the mortuary guys, of course, were all experts at death. They'd seen and heard wailing before. They knew how to keep their faces neutral, likely having rehearsed it in the bathroom mirror. They knew to wait, to see if I would collapse or recover.

I followed them down the hall to Jim's room. Counting one, two, three, they lifted what had used to be Jim onto a narrow cart and strapped it down. One last gurney ride for all those cancer cells that so determinedly murdered their host. I was relieved to see that there was no discolored body-fluid dampness on the mattress.

When the men got the cart to the base of the steps, I remembered moving a new TV down the stairs with Jim for him to watch while sick from chemo. It was one of the first high-definition sets, before TVs got slender. More than three feet wide and two feet deep, it weighed in at 190 pounds. "We've got gravity working for us going down, but this monster will never leave," I'd laughed as we slowly bumped the set down one step at a time.

Jim's corpse weighed more than that TV. The portly guys looked at the steep stairs and positioned themselves – one at the top of the steps and one at the bottom. Halfway up, gravity reared its head. Jim's body strained grotesquely against the restraints as the men struggled to get the cart up to the foyer.

While Pauline and I watched, the round man at the top tugged. The round man at the bottom heaved. The cart did not budge; Jim's body shifted. They paused to puzzle over the problem, holding the cart in place mid-stairs while scratching their crew cuts and working their fleshy jowls like Tweedledum and Tweedledee.

I impatiently scooted Tweedledum over and said, "You push on that side. I'll push on this one. Pauline, you push in the middle." I looked up at surprised Tweedledee at the top of the steps. "Now, all together, let's go." I put my shoulder to the gurney with the hysterical strength of a mother who lifts the car off her child and rammed the cart up the stairs. I was getting that dead body out of the house.

In a few minutes the hearse turned around and pulled out of the drive. I let the dogs go in a raucous frenzy and closed the door. Pauline was standing next to me. Readiness to help was shining in her eyes, but I desperately needed to be alone. To my surprise, when I asked her to go, she packed up to leave as willingly as she agreed to come. Then I opened the back door and let in the explosive dogs. Lila and Digs whirled around me and rushed downstairs and back, sniffing the strangeness in anxious concern. I sank to be with them on the floor, running my hands over Lila's solid body and putting up with her licks. Jim's dog, Diggity, was standoffish and peeved.

* * *

It was a luxury to take a shower without worrying that Jim had fallen, to not open the medical notebook to check drug dosages, to be upstairs away from the dying zone. Bone-tired from being up all night, numb from Jim's last hours and death, but still buzzing, I walked into the kitchen. Last night's soup was partly dried onto the cups that had been thrown into the sink during his seizure. I picked up the goopy cups and tossed them into the trash. I opened the refrigerator and poured the rest of the blended soup down the disposal, its whir matching the one I felt inside. Dull and dazed, I sat at the ugly mustard-colored kitchen counter. From my deep recesses came a desire for a list. A shiny new list to guide my blinking brain. I would be fine if I had a list so that I could check things off. So that I could move forward. Phone friends. Call work. Cancel Jim's appointments. Mail his letter to his sister. And most importantly, hand out the frogs.

This was what Jim wanted me to do after he died – not mope around the house or wash his corpse, but hand out the frogs. To a half-dozen people who had been especially helpful over the last year and a half. Jim and I had decided on a gift – a bowling-ball-size frog garden sculpture – not a silly frog with a smile, but a decent, mossy green replica of a frog. It was Jim's droll way of saying good-bye.

I began to smile as I remembered the rehearsed script we had worked up: *Jim died this [fill in morning, afternoon, or evening]. I have something that he wanted me to bring you. When would be good?*

My daughter, Emily, had cancelled her trip and was driving down from Indianapolis; I could get all the frog-delivery appointments made, and we could deliver frogs together. She would love doing it. I imagined us out driving the neighborhoods playing this little prank. Just like Jim planned, it would be fun in a gruesome way. It was Saturday; I'd be able to catch most people at home.

And checking things off my list, we could mail the letter to Jim's sister and take Jim's obituary and documents to the funeral home to Tweedledum and Tweedledee as promised. At that my stomach took a dive – I had to write the obituary. And I had to get it done before Emily arrived; she was on her way.

While waiting for the computer to boot up, the buzz began to race in my chest – it was hard to draw a breath. Fighting off self-induced suffocation, I looked out the window to the gray and white birds flitting around the feeders under the silver maple and mechanically forced myself to pull air into my lungs. *Inhale slowly, count to five, exhale slowly while counting to eight.* Soon the dark-eyed juncos would be gone, off to a different life in western mountains. Soon the creeping thyme that stretched down the fence almost to the bog would bloom; its deep pink flowers would blanket the ground and its lemon scent would release at my step, not caring if Jim were here or not.

I poised my fingers above the keyboard. Today I would quit typing in names of drugs or searching for information on care of the dying. With luck I would never again look up cancer survival rates. I ran my index finger across the keys. Where to start? Jim's instructions had been to write a sparse obituary and to have no services, but he didn't specify the other details. Good thing he wanted something simple, because I was in no shape for complex.

Just basics. Name, date, age. Graduation from Indiana University. His work on the pipeline in Alaska and in the factory, his time as a machine gunner in Vietnam – a mention of his Purple Heart. Would he be unhappy with me for including it? "It's nothing more than an award for being stupid enough to get shot," he used to say. But no mention of his inventions; that would be too personal.

Next, family. His dead parents, and using that charged phrase, *survived by* his sister and – my fingers hovered for a moment before typing – *wife*. I still wasn't used to that term. The only place I had been Jim's wife was with doctors and nurses and at my job, for our marriage had been a secret. Mostly secret anyway. I had told a few people, my family, a couple friends; he had told his sister, old girlfriends who still called.

Last week, when Jim was instructing me on what to do after he died, he'd laughed, "Imagine how shocked people will be when they find out we're married!" People would be shocked. I was still a little shocked myself that we had done it. Well, the cat was coming out of the bag now, but instead of a wife, I was a widow.

I pushed the print button as Emily pulled into the driveway, not realizing I had misspelled Jim's middle name. Later, the obit would have to be reprinted and the death certificate reissued. I also forgot to include that Emily was his step-daughter and picked a photo that printed fuzzy. I should have waited, gotten some sleep, and double-checked the documents, but I didn't. It had to be done right then, an essential element in getting death out of the house.

Lila stood at the picture window and wagged her tail as Emily popped open the hatchback to retrieve her suitcase. My daughter, one of the few people in this world whom Lila trusted, had put a hold on her life and was staying with us for two weeks. Digs barked sharply, hyped up as if she had the buzz too.

Emily has always been an antidote to my busy. Of everyone in the world, she knows how to handle my intense need to organize and make progress. She has an easiness about her that I lack, and the insane buzz that droned under my skin needed some easing.

"Oh, Momma," said Emily as she wrapped her arms around me, letting the vastness of her calmness neutralize my jagged buzz. "We're going to miss him so much, but thank heavens it's finally over."

I lingered in her warm hug and let myself sink a little into her comfort. Then I rallied, saying, "Here's the plan." I quickly outlined our afternoon of frog and funeral home appointments. "If I can get this done, I'll be fine."

She stood back, momentarily amazed. Then she wiped her eyes and said, "It will be good for you to get away from the house. The sun is out and it's supposed to get up to fifty degrees. Let's load up the frogs, and the dogs too." She reached down and petted Lila's smooth, eager head while Diggity nervously bumped and snorted against her.

It worked out just as Jim and I had planned.

While Emily and girls looked on from the curb, I knocked on the doors.

Each time, the unsuspecting frog recipient opened the door sadly, thinking I was there to grieve with them.

Instead, in both hands I'd offer one of the mossy frogs while saying with a smile, "Jim wanted you to have this for helping him while he croaked."

Taken aback, they'd look at the frog, puzzle, and then they'd get it. A perfect postmortem absurdity in true Jim style.

*   *   *

No funeral, no services, cremate me. Jim had made me promise over and over.

"That doesn't mean I can't throw a big party," I'd said back to him and to Emily when we got back home. "Let's invite everyone. Have ham sandwiches and Budweiser. That was his signature meal. We can make a Jim museum in the lower level of the house. His Purple Heart and Vietnam stuff, his cat and horse drawings, the sculptures of hands, his old black scuba mask. Put out some inventions – a Dog-Proof Cat Feeder with the patent papers, the Vasculator, Ape Arms, the 3D map of the Deam Wilderness."

"Put out his metal and wood puzzles," Emily said, joining in. "Load the CD player with Jim's favorites."

A rush of names flowed through me as if a dam had broken. "Yes, Roy Orbison, Bob Dylan, John Lennon, the Moody Blues, John Prine, Enya, the Grateful Dead, Pink Floyd."

"Don't forget Madonna, Annie Lennox, Paul Simon, and Elton John," said Emily.

The flow in my brain broadened. "And important books. I'll have to find them in the boxes out in the pole barn."

I pulled my parka around me as I walked into the chilly barn. I opened the heavy door to Jim's silent workshop. The most recent model of his Ape Arms project, a strapped-on device to extend arms to the ground so that humans scamper through the woods as easily as apes, was sitting disassembled on his workbench. This model, built while Jim's brain was betraying him, was a mess. I could see him sitting there, knowing that his work was wrong but not knowing what to do. I could feel the weight of the books stored above me. I found an earlier version of the Ape Arms model that made more sense to take inside.

I closed the door, my heart heavy, and set the model down. Then I angled my light-aluminum ladder against the side of the workshop to get to the storage area above. With dread, I hoisted myself up to where the boxes awaited me.

There they were. All of our lost conversations stacked in the attic. I wanted only two books, but to find them I had to pry open the top flaps of a dozen cardboard boxes, saddened by seeing Jim's scrawly handwriting on each. Growing more numb and buzzy with each box and slightly high from the sour mildew, I opened, closed, stacked, and restacked until I found the old formative books. *Catch-22* because he loved its paradoxical, satirical circular logic. *The Painted Bird*, the book he had read over and over until short-term memory returned after his big Alaskan accident. I sat back on my haunches and looked at the left-behind books, feeling like I could crawl inside one of the forlorn boxes and be right at home.

* * *

Mid-week, people packed the house – both levels, his and mine – late into the night, music cranked up. Jim's invited sister didn't come, of course. We partied down and let him go. But it didn't make me feel any better. It didn't quiet the buzz. Like yellow jackets burrowing under the siding of a house, it was in every fiber of my being – in the porous network of my bones, in the hundred billon neurons of my brain, in the tiny hollow sacs of my lungs. It even beat against the elastic membranes of my eardrums, adding a constant low-level hum to every moment.

I wanted to be in shredded black rags, wandering in a shrieking wind on a moonless night. I wanted to cry, crazy like a loon. I wanted to go to bed and never get up. But instead I was dry-eyed with this unwanted surging inside. Maybe it was the pent-up force that I had mustered for so long to research his disease, negotiate the medical system, and take care of Jim's every need, now so suddenly unneeded. Instead of weeping, I found myself inappropriately smiling and laughing. Thirsting for release from the horror of his illness, I tackled getting rid of his bed, his clothes, his gun, his reading chair, and his couch. Emily stuck by my side, never once suggesting that we slow down or take it easy. I think she was hoping I would play myself out.

Two days after the party, I paced through the almost empty rooms of the lower level, ravenously eating a piece of pizza. Empty pizza boxes were scattered on the industrial blue carpet, and Emily was sitting on a Jim-made coffee table that had been spared during the great purge. We'd run out of leftover ham sandwiches and defaulted to pizza. I walked down the hall, pausing to look at the bathroom. "I hate this bathroom. Who would ever put in a yellow plastic shower and toilet? Look at this painted-over, buckled wallpaper." I stuffed the rest of the pizza into my mouth and walked down the hall to Jim's bedroom, empty except for his desk and a bookshelf that had also managed to avoid the trip to the dump. There was a triangular, flame-shaped section of white wallpaper that had been ripped off to expose the underlying dark paneling.

"I hate this whole trashy house. Every inch of it needs to be replaced," I shouted down the hall.

"Want another piece of pizza?" Emily shouted back.

I wiped my greasy lips with the back of my hand while I returned to the living room. "No, save some for breakfast." I sat down next to Emily and tossed pieces of crust to the circling dogs. "I hate my life. I don't want to live here. I want to sell the house and quit my job. Maybe drop out of marketing and go work in a bookstore."

"Maybe you should wait a little bit before you make such big decisions," said Emily. "You don't have to decide anything right now."

"I want to change things right now." I ran my fingers over the table's heavy brass grate inset.

"Maybe you should remodel," she suggested. "It would make it easier to sell the house if you wanted. Replace those kitchen counters like you've been planning. You could convert Jim's room to your office."

*   *   *

"I can barely move," I said to Emily as I sank onto the plastic drop cloth a few days later. From hand to elbow, from nose to toe, I was streaked with sticky drips of faux paint glaze. "Whew, that glaze nearly did me in. It's harder to do than they say. Do you think this color was a mistake? Does it look fleshy?" I'd had trouble with fleshy before, once painting a whole house a light peach only for it to look like pale skin.

"It's not fleshy," laughed an equally paint-splattered Emily. "It's like crème brûlée or those pale tiger lilies you have in the garden by the patio. It will look different when it's dry."

She extended a hand to me. "Here, get up with me."

We linked hands and used our weight to pull each other up.

"Turn around," said Emily." See how different the room looks? The one terra-cotta-colored wall and three light creamy ones. It changes everything. It's not Jim's room anymore."

"I hope you're right." I spun slowly with her and then stopped to see the setting sun through the window high in the wall. "See the cardinals clustered at the feeder?" I pointed them out to Emily. "And how the sun halos the white sycamore tree at the edge of the dark woods by the bog? This is a good spot for my big oak table."

"See, you'll love working in this room."

I let myself linger briefly in Emily's smile and then leaned my head onto her welcome shoulder until the fear of paint drying in the trays and my ricocheting buzz roused me to action. I minced my way across the plastic sheeting between splatters and roller trays to pick up a paint can. "I need to clean up."

Emily nodded. "Before I leave for home in the morning, we can bring down the rug to throw over the carpet and move everything down here. Your bookcases and table. Your file cabinets. Your computer."

At the mention of her leaving, I felt the buzz gather strength and hoarsely whisper a promise of madness. I was tired of putting it off, wallowing in Emily's good cheer and safety. I wanted to give in, to see what the buzz held in store for me. I was ready to indulge myself with an unfettered free fall. I had two weeks before I had to go back to work.

The next afternoon, I closed the door behind Emily and descended into the buzz. Days without seeing or hearing another human, the buzz's energy fueled a newfound and all-consuming obsession to make the house I so hated habitable. The worried dogs trailed me as I wandered the two levels and made plans to get in control. I would start by tearing out the bathroom, pulling up the carpets, replacing the kitchen countertops and sink, and beating back the wraiths by replacing the surrounding acres of lawn with sweeping gardens of blazing color.

6

Line of Salt

I needed to catch my flight and was late for the ferry. Driving alone and fast in an open-air Jeep, under a grimy, crumbling, rebar-exposed concrete overpass by a dirty river. I knew I'd taken this route before with Jim to go scuba diving. I was wearing his red-and-white-plaid flannel shirt.

Then the Jeep quit running. A leering, watery-eyed guy in a farmer's cap gave me a ride in his pickup. He pulled up to a big ferry landing. When I tried to pay him forty dollars for the ride, he took out a pistol. I wasn't worried; I knew he wouldn't shoot me, because he never had before. But he shot me dead.

Jim strolled up with a wide smile. His jeans, T-shirt, and plaid flannel shirt hung loosely on his rangy frame. He looped his long arm around my back and pulled me to him, "Hey, babe, what's new?"

"I'm dead," I said, still surprised.

"I know," he said. "I'm here to save you."

"From what?"

"Yourself," said Jim with an irresistible Street-Car-Named-Desire-Marlon-Brando sultry smirk. Hand on my elbow, he steered me to a bar in a low-slung, pale, concrete block building in the vacant, littered riverfront. A glowing red neon Budweiser sign over blacked-out windows. A heavy door with a porthole window. Inside, grinning, yellow-toothed hellos from all the hard-living boozers we had known who died young. Some gaunt, some burly. They hung lazily over worn wooden tables, empty beer cans askew, ashtrays overflowing with bent, snubbed-out butts.

Jim magically produced two cans of cold Budweiser.

"Here's to being saved," I said, clinking my can to his.

"You know, once you get really dead, you can't get drunk anymore," Jim said in a low Leonard Cohen voice. "Talk about hell; none of us will ever be drunk again, but we have nothing to drink but beer." He took a long pull on his can.

"But I feel a buzz."

"Well, that's because you're freshly dead. When you get more dead, you can't get buzzed anymore."

Knowing he didn't understand that the kind of buzz I had would never go away, I reached over and touched Jim's ever-luscious, rock-hard bicep, trailing my fingers languidly down bulging veins to the inside of his wrist.

"I can't feel that either," he said. "You slowly lose all sensations, too."

Looking directly into his eyes, I leaned across the table and lightly took his soft, thick bottom lip in my teeth and moved my hand across his jeans to his crotch. "How about this? Can you feel this?"

There was a welcome stirring at my touch.

He pushed me away. "Nope, can't feel that," he said, eyes hard.

"Oh, well, who gives two shits? I'm glad to see you."

"Here's to that," he said, calling for a beer and a bump.

A bump? He never got bumps. He doesn't like whiskey.

Then I awoke, the scent and touch of Jim all around.

* * *

I could feel Jim around me most of the time. Sometimes I argued with him about where to put things in the pole barn. I'd find myself reciting my half of our standard jokes. Sometimes I felt his broad shoulder and long body in my bed. Sometimes his arm wrapped around my shoulder.

But mostly it was Jim's black-cloaked last days and death that gnawed at me. Images came unbidden. His crossed eyes. His seizures. The sadness of his incontinence. His death-bed struggle. Me being too busy to hold his last look. The awful pooling of his dead blood under his skin. I couldn't get away from them, they were like burdock burrs that work their way into fur. On my reinstated commute to work, on my walks in the woods, with evening glasses of wine, and, worst of all, in the room where he died.

The spot was just over my left shoulder as I sat at the desk in my office. All that was really there was my filing cabinet, a basket of magazines on Jim's rotating encyclopedia table, and in a cheerful, beaded frame a goofy photo of him peering over a black and orange box turtle. But it felt like an apocalyptic black hole of death, a vortex of horrible whirling behind my back while I sat working at the computer. It made it hard to focus on the projects I brought home from work as I tried to regain a grip on my job.

And then there were Jim's leftover ashes.

Jim had picked out a tubular sandstone container a few months earlier while shopping with me in a bead and rock store. "This is nice," he'd said, turning the hollowed-out cylinder over in his hands, tracing its smooth beige and tan sedimentary swirls. "Put my ashes in this."

Of course I'd bought that sandstone jar after he died. That wasn't the problem. It sat calmly in the window above my desk. The ashes that were causing the problem were the ones that didn't fit in the jar. Jim had underestimated how much of him would be left – enough to fill a shoebox, or about half of another sandstone jar. I'd scattered his ashes in all the typical places – where we liked to walk, favorite lunch spots in the woods, a handful into the lake. And still some were left. Emily took all she wanted. And still some were left. His sister refused to take any. They sat in the aluminum mortuary tin on my bookshelf like ignored regret. Every time the encyclopedia-table-black-vortex-to-hell began to spin like the girl's head in *The Exorcist* and the images of Jim's dying washed over me, the leftover ashes joined in.

I wished that the mysticism that makes many people feel protected would work for me, the undead. That a god, shrine, prayer, crystal, candle, potion, herb, or visualization would beat back these unseen evils. Keeping evil out of the house in the first place has long been established as easier than extracting it.

Memorial Hall, over on the Indiana University campus, a Gothic building with turrets over a heavy arched entry, has a quote from Sir Walter Scott: *Evil Spirits Cannot Enter An Inhabited House Unless Invited* carved in the limestone near the door that I used to walk through to my class on Eastern religions.

With red doors, the Chinese invite good luck and churches signify safe passage.

Lines of salt in the doorstep can't be crossed by demons until all the grains have been counted, a protectively impossible task.

Horseshoes, lion heads, feng shui mirrors, and Torah verses in decorative cases have long been hung by doors to prevent the crossing of bad energy over the threshold.

When the coyotes started jolting me from sleep every night, like banshees circling the house and planning to attack, their rusty-hinge yowls reverberating in the translucent pale moonlight over the frosted gardens, I decided to get some faux protection.

Packed away in the garage were cement-cast lion heads that had been bought in voodoo-laced New Orleans on a delirious, steamy August afternoon long ago with Jim. The heads used to hang by the doors of the house, one in back and one in front. But when Jim moved in, he made me take them down.

"Bric-a-brac. Things to run into and knock down," he'd threatened.

Maybe if he'd let them stay, he'd be alive; the cancer demons would have been frightened off at the door. I hung the fierce, pointy-toothed heads back up. I wasn't taking any chances.

I also took to wearing Jim's flannel shirts, ones I'd given him for Christmas and held back from giving to Goodwill. They didn't dispel the images of his dreadful dying, but it was like having his good, handsome, fierce strength spread over me. By my side, tall and buff, with big shoulders veeing to a narrow waist, his hands easy, I had always felt safe in Jim's company.

Now I felt so vulnerable. But I didn't know why.

After all, for most of my adult life I had not lived with him or any other man. I was an independent woman. A single parent, head of the household, senior manager, homeowner, maker of my own destiny. I wanted to return to that sure, brave, provocative woman. I didn't like myself as the jumpy, irrational, haunted weirdo I'd become.

Deep down, I felt broken.

I'd known illness and death, but not in this way. Not smashed right up against it along with the one who was dying. Forever my life would be divided into the time before Jim died and the time after. But I despised my bleak, shadowy madness for its self-pitying indulgence. After all, what I had done was nothing that hasn't been done by countless others who have nursed children, mothers, fathers, lovers, husbands, and friends who had died.

When I sought refuge in gardening catalogs, on- and offline, things felt better. How could irrational demons compete with such lyrical, hopeful paragraphs? "The show begins in early spring, when the large, oakleaf-shaped leaves unfurl a brilliant gold . . . eventually darkening to chartreuse and finally green just as the huge 6- to 8-inch white bloom trusses – giant snowy wands in the shade garden! – appear to liven things up again." Stacks of catalogs marked with neon Post-it notes multiplied like rabbits around my reading chair. I longed to sink my hands into black loam and walk down curving pathways between weedless garden beds. If I created the gardens, I thought, I would be cured.

It was my grandmother who taught me to find succor from the things I could not change in the patient, yielding soil of the garden. About being in the now with the pleasures of tomatoes plucked ripe off the vine and heavenly scented, luscious peony blossoms. She was the one who taught me to wait for the dark red fingers of peonies to poke up out of the spring soil. To watch for the day that the shiny green leaves burst up out of the crowns. To measure the advance of spring by the round, bulging buds as they grew as fat as green plums. To watch the big black ants nibble back the sweet edges of the sepals as the pink and red petals peeked through. *Pinies* she called them.

From the very beginning of my time on earth, I remember following her around in the garden. Photos show me as a big-cheeked toddler with stubby little legs in dark socks and solid shoes on the narrow backyard sidewalk that bisected her garden. I can almost put my finger into the light undulating across the surface of cool water in her silver galvanized bucket and hear the soft shushing of my grandfather cutting their small lawn with a reel push mower. Tender pink-and-white bleeding hearts bloomed merrily across from the kitchen doorsteps. Her orderly vegetable garden was hedged by pie-destined gooseberry bushes.

When I grew older, she took me out to slice through the base of crisp, ruby-tinged rhubarb with kitchen knives. Lopping off the huge poisonous leaves in the sink and chopping the celery-like stalks into cubes, we cooked up steaming bowls of tangy pink sauce.

On summer afternoons I would sit in the porch swing with my grandfather, running my finger over the thick crease in his thumb-nail while he taught me the *cheer-up, cheer-up* song of the robin and the *pretty, pretty* song of the cardinal. In the evenings we would drift slowly on the porch swing next to the trellis of honeysuckle, its sweetness flirting in the breeze, my drowsy head against my grandmother's shoulder, her hands clean and trimmed against her rick-rack-aproned lap.

I had always thought of my grandparents' house as a trouble-free haven and gave no thought to their difficulties or how death had pursued and wounded them. I rarely thought about the awful death of their son, an uncle I never met, and his girlfriend in an automobile accident when he was just twenty-four. It was a scandal – he had been drinking and was married to someone else. I never considered the loss of my grandfather's first wife to influenza in her early thirties, scattering their three children permanently to the homes of kin. Or of the tragic death of my grandmother's father, kicked by a horse and dying as he coughed up blood at the young age of thirty-four, resulting in near starvation for his three young daughters and widow.

These deaths were shattering catastrophes, not the passing of an older man after a full life. Yet my grandparents were the most peaceful, positive people I knew. Maybe it was their religion that made them so sure of life. Inside their slim New Testament, which I now have, is this poem written in my grandfather's hand:

Don't Wait
July 14, 1951

When I quit this mortal shore,
And mosey 'round the earth no more,
Don't weep, don't sigh, don't sob –
I may have struck a better job.
Don't go and buy a large bouquet
For which you'll find it hard to pay,
Don't mope around and feel all blue –
I may be better off than you.
Don't tell the folks I was a saint
Or any old thing that I ain't.
If you have jam like that to spread –
Please hand it out before I'm dead.
If you have roses, bless your soul
Just pin one on my button-hole
While I'm alive and well today –
Don't wait until I've gone away.

Alas, I have no such faith. I don't believe in spirits or ghosts, or gods, or destiny. I've wanted to. At various times I've been Presbyterian, Methodist, Episcopalian, Quaker, Buddhist. I've worked for the Lutherans and Catholics. I confess to eras of Tarot readings, astrological charts, I Ching penny tossing, and numerology reports. Once while I was self-employed, I had my fortune told in New Orleans. I had to laugh when the seer said, "You have problems with your boss." How true, I do have problems with myself. But the real hoot was the useless numerology online reading I read on the day Jim died: *Today is hectic, and it may be necessary for you to make quick decisions and put your leadership skills into action. Your senses are alert. Sounds, colors, and texture are strongly experienced.* Could have applied to a day at the zoo with a troop of girl scouts.

But I did have a garden that encircled my house, a garden that would protect me as well as any god. A place where I would be able to bury my self-pitying sorrows and the power of the demons that fueled the black vortex behind my shoulder in my downstairs office. Where the microbes of decay could work in my favor. I began wishing that I could piss, like a guy, along the edges of the property to keep the damned yowling coyotes and disaster at bay. And then it struck me: I could ring the property with Jim's extra ashes. Let him mark the boundary for me. It would be a no-trespassing line of salt-ash on the threshold of my territory.

The next time the vortex began to whirl, I tugged on my boots, zipped up my parka, picked up the partially empty cremation can, and went out the front door, hauling the black-cloaked demons with me. Late March snow outlined the arms of trees and sat in clumps on the green spruce boughs. The wind was still. I crossed over crunchy grass stubble to the property boundary by the icy bog, where a chorus of spring peepers frogs lay hibernating. The dogs followed, nose to ground, and then shot off to follow a track into the thicket.

I shoved my cold hand into the ashes and began to walk and sprinkle. The action was familiar. It was the same as sowing seed, only now it was an insane sowing of protection. Even strides, an even casting of granular Jim. The dogs returned and stuck with me, generally coursing along the path Jim had mowed last fall between the fence and the woods. A line of ash with demons expelled to the other side. Down one side, across the back, following the edge of the pasture out to the road, and around to the cluster of Norway spruce until I stood where I started.

At the bottom of the can, my fingers came across a ragged lump of metal. I thought it was dental work until I recognized its shape from the MRIs. It was the shrapnel that had been lodged next to Jim's clavicle, a bit of the Vietnam surviving him.

I dropped the shrapnel into my pocket and smacked the bottom of the can to be sure it was empty.

Inside the house, a hundred or so seedlings were spreading their embryonic leaves in six black plastic trays under fluorescent grow lights on the seed-starting stand in the dining room.

7

Drainage

Normal. All I wanted was to get back to normal, and I was sure I could find some of it hanging with my shovels or maybe in the drawer with the frost-proof netting in my potting shed behind the house. At the first brief spiking of late March temperatures, I kicked back the heaved-up mud from the bottom of the shed's heavy door and banged upward on the metal hook holding the latch until it gave way. The door swung open, and I was greeted by a hint of pungent spice, warmed in the unseasonable heat, from the forgotten, twine-tied bundles of sage and lemon thyme hung from the dark green rafters last fall.

Through the slanted southern window of the cold frame, I scanned the bare woods beyond the pasture for signs of spring. It was too early. Flaccid spiderwebs hung across the corners of the glass, and the wooden frame was askew and slightly buckled. An early wasp darted in mild menace, protecting the beginning of a geometrical nest tucked behind the antique hand scythe on the wall. A winter's accumulation of grime and dead balls of roly-poly bugs littered the top of the potting bench. I loved the colors in here – the dark green bench and the creamy mint-green walls, softened in the light coming through the slanted opaque roof. My glance moved from a small puddle of water to a wet seam where the skylight roof joined shingles. I made a mental note to caulk the roofline.

I ran my hands across the work surface of the L-shaped bench, brushing the debris to the gravel floor. The filmy veil of Jim's last look appeared and drifted by. This was where Jim had once knelt, measuring me from bent elbow to the ground so that the bench would be a perfect height for me.

But it wasn't a romantic or sentimental gesture; it had been part of his plan to get me and my stuff out of the pole barn. Jim had wanted the pole barn for himself – his private workshop, a place where the guys could hang out with the garage doors open, smoking and drinking beer, with no sign of a woman anywhere. A place where he could retreat in case cohabitation with me was overwhelming, in case he needed more than his own private floor in the house. Not that I could blame him; blending our lives had been scary for me too. In fact, using the excuse of needing a place to offset the brutality of my long commute, I had bought a condo escape in northern Indianapolis. Worse than marking off the pole barn as private territory or dividing the house into two separate levels to live, I had a whole other place to live, just in case. That condo had gone nearly unused until Emily moved into it but the same could not be said of Jim and his pole barn.

To persuade me to move my tiller, gardening tools, bags of dirt, tomato cages, bean stakes, and stacks of clay pots away from the pole barn's comforts of electricity, running water, and dry concrete floor, Jim had convinced me that a small red barn behind the house would make a perfect potting house and garden shed. He would rebuild it to my specifications.

It didn't take much convincing. I'd had a garden shed, deep cold frame, and potting bench at my house before this one and knew exactly what I wanted. Jim quickly drew up plans to convert the barn. We would jack up the building, pour cement for new footings, and rebuild the walls.

The old chicken coop winging out on one side would become a potting shed. The high-raftered Dutch gambrel main barn would become a storage area. The old horse paddock winging out on the other side would become a covered west-facing patio (ultimately to become the Sunset Lounge, named tongue-in-cheek after a rowdy Bloomington bar long demolished). We would rip off the rusted metal roof over the wings and replace it with translucent polycarbonate panels.

Outside the cold frame window I saw that the black locust tree in the pasture had dropped several large branches over the winter. I idly wondered if I should learn to use a chain saw. According to my neighbor, who had farmed all the land along the road, this once had been a locust grove. You could still see it enduring everywhere, if you looked. The old fence posts were locust, some still sprouting leaves each year. The extremely hard and rot-resistant wood had been favored by farmers before the proliferation of steel posts. Locust trees bordered the pastures; one had even been growing in the wall of the barn. Their elongated clusters of creamy-white flowers scented air in late spring with an intense fragrance. But that sweetness belied their nasty invasiveness, finger-shredding thorns, and proclivity to shed branches in storms. They fought to reclaim their old groves by pushing up spiky saplings from malevolent and persistent underground root networks in my vegetable garden.

The old, original corner post of the chicken-coop-turned-potting-shed was a round, barkless tree trunk, probably locust. When Jim and I had started the garden shed project, this support beam and the whole barn were severely tilted. It had been my idea to nudge the building upright with the pickup truck.

"It will never work," Jim had said. "The truck will get stuck in the pasture. It's always soft and wet. If you hit the barn with the truck, you'll knock it down."

But I had walked the pasture. I knew that the soggy areas dried up in the August drought, making the ground under the locust tree relatively firm. "We don't have to ram into the barn, just push it gently," I'd said. "I'll do it."

Gamely, Jim agreed. "If it falls down, it's your fault."

Thrill pounded in my chest as I drove the truck off the asphalt, behind the pole barn, and up the pasture to the ramshackle building.

"Now comes the hard part," Jim said after I parked the truck under the tree, nose toward the barn. "The bumper has to touch the beam just right."

I shifted the body of the truck back and forth several times, feeling it sink into the field with each adjustment. The rear tires spun, then caught and shot forward. I tapped the brake and slid, kissing the thick corner beam with front edge of the truck. The building shuddered.

Jim signaled with his fingers for me to nudge the truck forward. "Slow, go slow."

There was traction under the tires. Ever so slowly, the barn straightened. Jim threw up his hand for me to stop and moved into fluid motion like a dancer, tossing two-by-fours up into an angled support scaffold to stabilize the barn, easily swinging his long framing hammer to slam home nails.

"Yes!" I shouted. I put the truck into reverse and the rear tires started to spin. I instinctively turned the wheel sharply. The truck slid clear of the both the barn and the tree and bounced down the long pasture back to the driveway. I didn't dare stop; there was water under that soil, even in August.

I learned later that groundwater springs dotted the saturated rise behind the house. Water was channeled away in two long, shallow ditches that had been dug by the previous owners. One swale was at the top of the rise in the flat of the back pasture, and one ominously curved a few feet away from the tar-coated block foundation of the house. If this property had never been made into pasture, never subdivided into a building lot, you'd find cheery buttercup-yellow marsh marigolds growing in a wetland under a scattered canopy of trees. Undisturbed mesic circumneutral seeps are groundwater-fed, pH-neutral wetlands that are considered rare in Indiana, but this property was plenty disturbed, just like me. Not all of our property was boggy, just certain sections. And where the water wanted to pool, I lived.

For fun I had once stuck my pH soil tester into the water, expecting to find it slightly alkaline from flowing through limestone karst, but the needle swung to a neutral pH. This was confirmed by the dogs, who dug a water bowl in the hillside for the especially tasty water that bubbled up out of the ground and rejected the chlorinated, fluoride-laced water from the house.

Jim and I hadn't known we were buying a seep. The ground was frozen when we bought the house. The only hint was the muddy garden clogs left behind in the garage by the previous owners, who never brought up the soggy subject. A note in the buyers inspection report, "Deeper swale needs cut in backyard," was our first clue, but it seemed like nothing compared to replacing the roof, a whole new heating and cooling system, rebuilding the chimney, building the workshop, and getting my stuff out to the converted barn.

Reality began to trickle in right after we bought the place when we fenced a half acre behind the house for the dogs. Plenty of room to race full-out with spots to catch the breeze or get out of the wind, for cool napping or to bask in the sun. The slope was good for belly rubbing, and the low branches of the white pines made good back scratchers. Dog Paradise we called it. It was the first project after buying the house – 450 feet of welded wire fence, 30-plus metal posts, and five wooden gates with supports sunk into cement. Our posthole digger hit water all across the top of the back hill. No need to haul water to mix with the cement, just empty the bag into the hole. *How handy,* we'd thought.

I glibly focused on how the seep would change my gardening. I was fascinated with it from a horticultural viewpoint – hunting for plants that liked wet feet but could stand to be drier during August – willow, hibiscus, corkscrew rush, blue flag iris. But when I gave

Jim Saturday tours of my young seepy gardens, he saw only the disquieting way the water lingered near the house.

Jim became a full-fledged water worrier upon his move into the house the autumn of his lung surgery, a long year and a half earlier. "I've been watching when it rains," he told me one night after work. "Water pools behind the house, just a few feet from my bedroom. Redigging the swales has to move to the top of our to-do list."

A reasonable person would have rented or hired a backhoe to deepen the swales. But Jim didn't. Just a few weeks after major surgery, he dug them out by hand. This was no little job. The swales were both at least a hundred feet long, together half the length of a football field.

For a full week I'd come home after work to be greeted by an exhausted and mud-covered Jim. He would proudly flex his biceps to prove that lung surgery meant nothing to him. "It's just like digging foxholes," he'd said. "Khe Sanh all over again. Water, the enemy, is everywhere. You just can't see it."

"I can see that you are crazy to do this," I'd complained, pointing to the shovel-wide ditches with high-heaped shoulders of wet, heavy, cold circumneutral muck. "These narrow channels might move the water, but this one that bisects the yard behind the house is an ankle breaker. And how will we mow around it?"

"I know," Jim had said. "I'll broaden it later. This will get the water away from the house for now, so I can relax."

But the deeper swales did not soothe Jim's water worries for long. Post-chemo, his concerns had swollen again.

"I've been living downstairs all winter thinking about what would happen if the wall springs a leak, about the hydrostatic pressure of all that water under the hill," Jim had grumbled.

"There's no sump pump," I'd said, shaking my head in reluctant agreement. "You know that old saying, 'It's not whether or not the basement leaks, it's whether or not the sump pump works.'"

"But I think there's an old drain." Taking me into the laundry room, Jim had pointed to a round indention in the floor. "Here, under the linoleum."

In a few days, out of the drain we had uncovered wafted a most foul odor. Jim stuffed a small red rubber ball into the drain, and said to me, "It's a brilliant solution. Works in two ways. Seals the stink, and will float up in a flood."

Unimpressed, I Googled *stinky drain* at work during lunch, and said to Jim as I poured myself a glass of wine that night, "Guess why S-traps are called S-traps."

"Because of their S-like shape, of course," said Jim.

"Wrong! It's because they trap sewer stink – the S is for stink," I crowed, tongue-in-cheek. "The water collects in the bottom loop of pipe. It blocks the smell of the stinky sewer gas. If the loop dries out, the stink comes in."

"So do you think we have an S-trap?" asked Jim, narrowing his eyes over his wine goblet.

I emptied the last of my wine. "Of course we do. Who would put in a drain without an S-trap?"

"Well, Little Miss Smarty Pants, why is our S-trap stinking?"

"Because it's dry. It's cracked."

"No," said Jim, harrumphing. "There's no S-trap. That's why it won't hold water. I'll put a bet on it."

"Bet it is," I said, extending my hand to seal the deal. Then, following our long-standing protocol, we both signed our names under our traditional pledge: "To these positions we commit ourselves. Five dollars to be paid to the one who is clearly correct."

The sealed envelope was still in the junk drawer in the kitchen. Trap or no-trap had gotten lost in the mire of surgery, radiation, and dying that engulfed us in the months that followed, and that stupid red ball was still plugging the drain. It was time to collect on my S-trap bet.

I knew that my neighbor's son had built the place. I had just hired his heating and cooling company to install aluminum dryer exhaust hoses (another thing on the long list of things that needed to be fixed). He would know about the trap. I dialed his number on the downstairs phone, staring intently at the drain in the laundry room.

"Sure, there's an S-trap," he said as I congratulated myself. "But it probably needs to be replaced."

Layers of concrete dust and a deep hole in the laundry room floor later, my premature congratulations soured.

"I would have sworn I put a trap in there," said my house's creator, pushing back his baseball cap and scratching his head. "I can't believe it."

"Neither can I," my stomach turning, knowing I'd have to pay back Jim.

Paying back Jim had always been dicey, and I wondered what he would extract from me this time, especially since money doesn't cross the border between the dead and the living. Maybe he didn't have anything to do with what was coming next, but I was about to become a water worrier on a torrential scale, way more than an unpaid five-dollar bet would be worth, and I held him responsible.

At first I thought Jim was extracting payment from me when the pipes burst in the pole barn in early April. But when images began to haunt me of the lower-level walls growing damp and water soaking the carpet, I knew he wasn't finished. After each big storm I would go down to my where-Jim-died office and check the walls and baseboards for dampness. I had become the water worrier.

It rained, it seemed, every other day for all of April and May. It wasn't long before I had French drain estimates spread out across my new, not-yellow, forest-green kitchen counter (a color suggested by Jim). I would do it right. Unlike crazy foxhole digging, I would have a perforated plastic pipe wrapped in a root-proof fabric and laid in gravel installed.

My still-buzzy brain wasn't making good decisions, and I couldn't decide what estimate to choose. It wasn't straightforward. They were all slightly different solutions ranging up to thirty thousand dollars. I had just logged onto my bank account to see how much I had in savings when the lights flickered and the computer switched to battery. The room went dark. The vent flap in the stove hood rattled in the wind.

I lit the kerosene lamp and didn't think much about it. It was a regular thing for the electricity to go out during storms. Lila and Digs were not as complacent; they were nervous, glancing over their shoulders at every thunder boom. My cat, Cirrus, sat on the back of the couch and rotated her ears like radar scanners. I peered out the side window and saw nothing in the pitch black. Wind-propelled whirligigs from the silver maple peppered the glass in the yellow lamplight.

Then I heard it. The legendary freight-train roar of a tornado. Others had told of it, but I had never heard it myself. It was like a ghost train from hell right out in the yard. The dogs whined and hid. There was a ripping, cracking noise.

You're supposed to go hide in a windowless basement, bathroom, or closet when a tornado comes, but I never have. That night I stepped out the front door into the black. The wind sucked my breath away as if I had walked into a vacuum. Just as I thought the closet under the stairs might be a good retreat, the air relaxed and the lights came on. The security light resumed its eerie illumination of Dog Paradise. I turned on the outside spotlights. Everything looked in order. The rains lightened, the dogs yawned, and Cirrus lazily strolled off to bed.

In the dim light of early morning, I whipped out of the garage to hurry to work. As I turned around in the drive, a large mass of misplaced green at the edge of Dog Paradise caught my eye. I stopped mid-driveway, got out, and tiptoed in my heels through the mushy lawn to investigate. It was a downed white pine. This had been the cracking noise. The wind had twisted it out of the ground, danced it across the grass, and laid the tree directly on top of a long fence line.

A sense of overwhelming hovered above me, taking shape like a damp mass. It started to form up and then lost its bulk as I picked up my cell phone to call a tree trimmer friend. When I hung up I said out loud to myself, "There. I can have my own personal tornado and handle it. No problem."

The freight-train storm was nothing. An insignificant sprinkle compared to the black hordes of thunderstorms that stomped through the next week like giants on the march.

The deep ditches Jim had dug were rushing wild like snow-fed mountain streams. One night after I'd battled my long commute home, peering through heavy rain that rendered the windshield wipers nearly useless, I discovered a growing pool of water around the back patio drain, making its way to the doors of the house and garage.

I hadn't thought about this. Water coming in under the doors, flooding the garage and foyer, cascading down the stairs to the lower level, making a carpet bog before finding its way to the newly reconstructed trap drain. Worry collected when I checked the online overnight weather forecast. Computer-generated green blobs with yellow and deep orange centers loomed on the maps just west of the county. Rain pelted the windows and thunder drove the dogs under my desk.

I switched on the back patio light and saw that, sure enough, the water was creeping toward the house. It looked like it was already against the garage door. I walked into the connected garage, where a long puddle had reached the tires of my Honda Element and a wet spot was blooming up the dry wall. I walked out to the patio and stood under the protection of the deep eave overhang, rain misting my glasses. Just a couple more inches and the water would be up to the door that opened to the foyer.

Paralyzed, the water inching toward me, I ran my hand over my face, unable to make a decision about what to do. As if somehow compassionate, the storm paused, the water receded, and the buzz that still resided in my cells pushed unresponsive me aside and took over.

I squeegeed the water out the front doors of the garage and moved everything away from where the fingers of water had invaded. Plastic sheeting over the bottom of the door held in place with the recycling bins – maybe that would work. But that was horse-out-of-the-barn thinking. I had to keep the water from reaching the doors in the first place.

The patio was surrounded by a low brick wall that contained the pool. What if I threw the water over the wall? Got it out of the patio?

When I awoke in the morning, it wasn't raining yet, but on my computer screen a storm front covering all of Illinois and half of Indiana was churning. I called work, my mouth dry, hardly able to speak. "Storms are forecast all day. I can't make it. I have to keep the water from coming in the house, from going down the stairs," I tried to explain to voice mail. "I hope I can make it in tomorrow. I'm calling the plumbers as soon as they open. I can work from here in between storms." I could sense the weariness of me and my problems on the other end of the line even though I was talking to a machine.

The gal who answered the plumbing company phone apologized. "I am so sorry, but it'll be two days before we can get out there. It's the best we can do. These heavy rains are causing everyone trouble. We're swamped," she said with the driest of humor.

Finishing the last of my coffee, I hung up the phone, walked down to the foyer, and stepped out the door to the patio. The pool around the drain had almost emptied overnight. The temperature was rising, the humidity was thick, and dark clouds boiled in the sky. Big splats of rain smacked down as the storm let loose. I backed up to the frame of the doorway under the eave and watched the pool swell.

I sighed. It was time to give bailing a try. I zipped up my grape-colored plastic raincoat and picked up the old pink bathroom waste-basket I'd found in the garage. Quickly I learned that a good toss could land water in Jim's ditch-now-stream on the other side of the brick wall. If I missed, the water hit the wall and splashed back into the pool that was filling the patio. I hit the ditch about three out of five tosses.

As I bailed, I saw that the drain was only part of the problem. Extra water poured into the low-lying patio from a garden pathway, dragging mulch with it to clog the drain. I realized this was my fault. Excavation dirt from a small wall I had built around the garden by the garage had raised the path. But that water was a dribble compared to the water now gushing over the gutters like Niagara Falls. I slicked my wet hair back. How had I lived here for more than four years without noticing that we needed wider gutters? Why had Jim missed this in his worrying investigations?

My sodden brain hatched a plan. "And it's a good one," I said aloud in case Jim could hear me. I could catch the gutter overflow in buckets to prevent pooling in the patio. During a break in the rain, I scrounged around the pole barn for plastic containers. Dumping out sand, ashes, ice salt, trash, and pinecones, I assembled a motley set of old kitchen wastebaskets, galvanized metal pails, cat-litter contain-ers, and five-gallon plastic buckets. I lined them up under the gutter, my perimeter line against the rain.

Bulky thunderheads rumbled black in the western sky as I prepped for the next battle. The plastic rain slicker was steaming me alive. Underneath, my clothes were sodden. I peeled off both the slicker and my clothes. I would fight in my underwear. "Okay," I said to the dogs, who stood anxiously watching me on the dry side of the door. "I've got this covered." I grunted, "Oo-rah," like a marine and brought my fist hard to my chest.

The rain made the next move. Fat drops followed by a barrage of undulating curtains. I bailed strategically, water over the wall to the ditch. For the first time, I held an even line against the water lapping at the garage door, or so I thought until I turned to see that Niagara Falls had filled the buckets under the gutters almost immediately.

This possibility had not occurred to me. I abandoned bailing, and started emptying the buckets over the wall. Easier said than done. How could I have forgotten? If one gallon of water weighs almost ten pounds, this means a five-gallon paint can weighs fifty – about the same as a big bag of mulch. I sloshed through calf-deep water and muscled the containers over the wall.

Bedraggled, in ratty underwear, winter-pale and lumpy, with no hope of backup help, I bailed all afternoon. On and off in the evening. In the middle of night. The storms rumbled in and out. My fingers were blue and wrinkled. The storms would not relent; they wanted me to let go first. But I couldn't; I had to save the house. Bailing, drinking wine, eating peanut butter sandwiches, completely alone in the country, I felt much the madwoman in my underwear, surrounded by the ever-filling, ragtag collection of Easter-colored plastic containers. But the buzz would not give in. Not to the storms and not to tears. I was the warrior against the world, and I would win.

Two days later I was still calling in to cancel work. But reinforcements were coming: the plumber, and a gutter guy too.

First the gutter guy. "Yep. You need wider gutters and another downspout. But we're backed up," he said with a straight face. "It'll be next week before we can get to it." I wondered what the seven-day weather forecast was.

John the plumber arrived in the afternoon. He seemed surprised to see me. "Didn't a guy used to live here?"

Jim's last look arose before me. "He died early this year," I said, looking away in hopes of avoiding another dead-Jim conversation. I tried to avoid bringing up dead Jim. Unlike when he was alive, I could hardly have a conversation without him in it. Jim used to say this. And Jim would have done that. And remember when Jim and I did this? Wouldn't Jim have liked that? And Jim loved to eat this. And Jim hated to go there.

"My regrets, ma'am," said John. "I remember him. A big guy, a tall drink of water. He brought me out here for an estimate to fix the downstairs drain and this one too. We talked about snaking a camera down the patio to see where it was draining. But he didn't want to do it. Said he'd take care of it himself. We talked about these gutters, too, and the swale around back here."

Stupid, I-can-figure-this-out-by-myself Jim had turned down John's practical suggestions and doomed me to this soggy insanity. *This* was me paying Jim back on that stinky S-trap bet.

John threaded a big rotor down the patio drain. It stopped after a few yards. In reverse, the rotor trailed long, yellow, mangled poplar roots out of the hole. We ran water from the hose to see if that fixed things; it seemed to drain.

"Call me if it quits working," he said.

When the storms returned around four in the afternoon, I watched the drain out the back-door window, hoping. The water circled around the drain, slowly but surely going down in little glugs. But when the rain got serious, the water began to pool. Soon I was sloshing in my underwear and bailing again, shouting, "Fuck you, Jim, for not having fixed this," with each bucketful.

The next day John returned with a fancy diagnostic video camera on the end of a flexible cable. He played out the cable down the patio drain. "It's stopped under that big poplar about twenty feet out and three feet down," he said pointing to a small monitor. "It doesn't really go anywhere. It just stops in the ground. It'd be a good idea to put in a new drain, one that empties into something besides compacted roots and dirt."

"Could you tie it into the ditches so that it drains into that?"

"Sure, but those ditches aren't going to last. You need a French drain."

"Yes, sir, I do," I smiled.

"We could do it for you, too, pretty reasonably. But we're so busy. It'll be a couple weeks before we can get to the patio and a couple months before we can dig you a French drain."

"What will I do? There's more rain forecast, and I have to go back to work. I can't stay here for another week and bail."

John hesitated before he spoke. "You can dig down to the underground pipe and bust a hole in it so that the water can run free. The pipe runs under the patio, under that garden, and over to the lawn. It angles down deeper as it goes. I can't do it, I have to go. You'll have to do the digging."

"I can do that. I'm strong."

"Yes, ma'am, I believe you can. If you can bail the water, you can dig the hole."

"Right here?" I walked over to the spot John had shown me before.

"Well, the equipment is not exact. The pipe could be two or three feet left or right." John smiled broadly as he gathered the last of his tools. "It's the best I can tell you. Good luck. I'll get you an estimate for the work we talked about."

I got the shovel and slammed it with the sole of my hiking boot into the wet ground and the fat, fleshy fingers of the poplar tree roots. I felt empowerment rush into me. And I felt buff. This bailing and digging was good for me. My back, legs and stomach, once strong from turning over garden beds, carrying rocks and bags of mulch, had grown flabby under the rule of Jim's illness. My body was hungry for work; it wanted to shed the layers of grief that had settled in my muscles.

The afternoon grew long, and the sky was leaden gray to the west. Orange clay, dense with yellow roots, piled high around me and a three-foot hole gapped before me. But no pipe. I leaned on the shovel. "Well, girls," I said to the amused dogs. "Should I dig to the left or the right?"

"We don't know," they grinned back. "But we are impressed. We didn't know it was okay to dig here."

"It's not okay for you to dig here," I said as I randomly chose the right. Embedded in the clay, several shovelfuls down, I unearthed a bright pink, Double Bubble gum wrapper. A clue! Humans have been at this level of the earth before. This is the direction.

I found the white PVC pipe and satisfyingly smashed into it with the shovel edge. Surprisingly brittle, it broke immediately and water gushed out. My adrenaline was pumping; the shovel dove into the clay and roots under my foot as if they were pudding as I finished a channel over to Jim's ditch another three feet away.

Exhausted, I felt the sludge of grief begin to shift. Grief that had started as a damp, black spot in my being when I read Jim's first pathology report almost two years ago: "adenocarcinoma with features of micropapillary and bronchoalveolar carcinomatous architecture at the tumor periphery."

I got a Rolling Rock from the refrigerator in the garage, twisted off the top, and took a long pull of icy relief. I sat on the short brick wall of the patio and toasted the ash-colored rain clouds moving fast through the atmosphere above me. "Screw you," I said to Jim. "We're even now."

8

Consilience

I invited the bug exterminator sales guy into the workshop as part of his introductory tour to look for signs of varmints in the house and the outbuildings – scatterings of mouse turds, mudded-over tunnels of termites, tangled telltale webs of black widow spiders – and that's when he started getting under my skin.

First he told me how grateful I should be for the discount he was giving me. I was willing to let that pass; he was just starting his new business and we knew each other, so maybe he really was giving me a discount. But right after that I got insulted.

"This kind of organization, this is what guys do," Mr. Exterminator said condescendingly as he stood before the tidy shelves of screws, nails, spray cans, paint cans, stains, drills, screwdrivers, hammers, and widgets of every sort. He pointed to a tube of Liquid Nails in the white plastic bucket of caulk guns and said, "Jim's."

I shut my mouth to be polite and escorted him to the garden shed at the back of the property. If I had opened my mouth, I would have said, "Who the hell do you think you are? You hardly even knew Jim. If you had known him, you horse's ass, you would know that he never used Liquid Nails. Jim was a real nails and screws man. I'm the wimpy one who uses Liquid Nails. What fucking right do you have assuming that an orderly workshop and Liquid Nails are here because of a man who died six months ago? I am not a witless inheritor of Jim's workshop."

Sure, Jim had piled tools and boxes in the workshop after his lung surgery, but it was me who had put all the bolts in one not-mixed-with-screws box. I was the one who had separated the Phillips-head from the Torx-head and the slotted-head screwdrivers. I had turned his scattered mess of sandpaper, electrical components, and magnets in weak-sided cardboard boxes into an organized affair in see-through plastic bins. True, I was all thumbs in my home repair attempts so far, but I was confident that would change.

Even little projects like making a wooden plaque to mount the house numbers seemed hard. I read and reread instructions for equipment. I looked stuff up online. I asked my friends. But my main source of hope was Kleindorfer's hardware store in town. It sits back away from the curve of the road that swings past the cemetery where Hoagy Carmichael, the composer of *Star Dust* and *Georgia on My Mind,* is buried. But you can't take the curve without seeing the store. It's painted a brilliant turquoise, and three lines of big, black, block lettering mirror the tiered shape of the storefront:

SAVE HERE!

KLEINDORFER'S

HARDWARE AND VARIETY STORE

People in Bloomington are devoted to Kleindorfer's almost forgotten hardware store tradition of a floor-to-ceiling inventory designed to be navigated with the help of people who know everything about how to fix anything. They not only know what doohickey you need but also can tell you what gadget you need to deal with the doohickey and what the instructions on the package don't tell you, and they do it all without making you feel like an idiot. And you don't have to buy a whole box of something when you only need one. Better than a husband and with a lower price.

When you walk in the door, past the wheelbarrows and wooden porch swings, there's a four-sided counter that operates like the central woodstove of old. Narrow aisles branch to the side and back. Right away someone in a flannel shirt asks if you need help. If you say no, they back off, and if you say yes, you really get help. Kleindorfer's puts out a coveted calendar each year with a bright photo of their landmark blue building on the cover and rugged wildlife photos – elk, bear, and wolf – at the top of each month. Except July, which gets the Statue of Liberty.

Bolstered by my Kleindorfer's backup arrangement, I tacked up a long-neck-beer girly poster I'd found in Jim's stuff (he'd never got around to putting it up, and what workshop is respectable without one?) and a chart of fraction and decimal conversions. Soon I would conquer a perfectly cut miter joint. Maybe I would even learn how to make furniture with interlocking dove joints. I would learn to run the table saw, just as soon as I could figure out how to change the blade. After all, I had done a wonderful job of organizing.

I should have given the bug guy a break, because so many women encourage men to think this way. I see such women in line at the big-box hardware store; eyes batting, head tilting, they say in their treble voices, "Oh, yes, could you carry that for me?" But Mr. Exterminator, here to judge the pest and decay level of the property, made me uneasy and unforgiving.

When we arrived at the garden shed, dogs barking viciously, Mr. Exterminator started clucking over how the bottom edge of the wood walls dangerously touched the soil, making it ripe for termites. He was right; that was bad. A couple of the lower planks of the door had rotted too. In fact the whole building was starting to revert to its former self. Wet had wiggled its fingers under the green paint inside and out, lifting flat flakes to reveal bare wood beneath. It had to be painted before another winter. I was lost in thought about the fifteen gallons of paint I had spread on the building during its original re-construction and what I hoped was the right process for getting the rotten planks off and new ones on when Mr. Exterminator cleared his throat to get my attention.

Tucking his clipboard under his arm, he pointed to the fire pit in the back pasture and gave a little manly advice to the poor widow.

"You should be careful burning fires there, especially if it's dry or windy," he scolded. As if I hadn't lived in wood-heated cabins and cooked on wood-heat stoves back in my hippie days. As if I hadn't burned a dead white pine tree in the pit just last week, one hand-sawed branch after another. As if I hadn't spent a whole day with Jim last fall burning his inventions in this very fire pit.

* * *

It was right after his brain surgery. Bleary-eyed one Saturday morning, I had looked out the kitchen window hoping to see the long rays of the morning sun striking the tulip poplars golden against the brilliant blue sky. Blocking my view was the pickup truck, Jim, and mounds of something in the pasture by the pit.

Coffee cup in hand, I walked up the slope to find Jim ringed by models, parts, and pieces of decades of inventing.

"What's going on here?" I asked, dreading his answer.

"Burning. I'm burning it all," he said, looking up at me from a box of widgets. "It's my stuff, and I can burn it if I want. You'll be glad I did. What would you do with a barn full of useless inventions?" Jim pushed back the baseball cap he wore to cover the stitches on the back of his head and smiled. "Wanna help?"

I walked toe to toe for a few feet, tamping down a mole tunnel, an empty argument against the burning swelling inside me. As I turned to protest, a plea in Jim's eye stopped me. He didn't want to argue; he wanted me to play with him.

"Sure!" I'd said, and then protested anyway. "Hey, you can't burn this." I nudged the original see-through clear plastic prototype of the Dog-Proof Cat Feeder with my toe.

"Watch me," he'd said in a wheezing grimace. "Damned cat feeders. What a disappointment. That was the million-dollar idea."

Jim turned and starting poking through a cardboard box of templates and spare parts. "Look at all this. I had to make everything. Each little part. All those hours we spent in hardware stores looking for parts no one made. I had to depend on rubber bands for the right spring action."

By the time the sun had dropped westward, the storage shelves in the pole barn were empty, except for a few sample models of Dog-Proof Cat Feeders. Several truckloads of inventions had been admired, photographed, dog-sniffed, and stacked in the pasture. It was a goofy landscape of the weird. Parts, pieces, models, and prototypes of Pooper Scooper, Electrostatic Map Holders, Ape Arms, Mantis Houses, and Push-Up Machines. In the fire pit a cushion of cardboard boxes supported a circle of multicolored Dog-Proof Cat Feeders.

Fatigue flickered across Jim's brow as he slowly wadded up his beer can, tossed it into the pit, and unscrewed the lid of the three-gallon red plastic gas can. Suddenly aware that the hours of hot ashes to come could easily begin to burn the pines or the garden shed, I scrambled down the hill to the house to get the hose, just in case, calling the dogs as I went. I quickly pulled the hose from its reel, up the grassy slope, and over the gate, shooing the dogs back.

Jim held the gas can aloft and toasted the heavens. "You motherfucker," he'd said. Then he shook big, dangerous splats of fuel onto the pile. It pooled in slick rainbows inside the Dog-Proof Cat Feeders and stained dark the cardboard boxes. The sharp smell of the shimmering vapors made me step back as Jim ignited a soaked rag and tossed it whooshing into the pit.

Long orange licks of black-rimmed flames whipped first toward the shed, then toward the pines, finally pulling into themselves as the gas burned off. The cardboard curled. The Dog-Proof Cat Feeders blistered, blackened, and burned. As did the 3D Drawing Machine and everything else we fed into the fire as the sunset blazed and then purpled.

Eventually I left Jim to this cremation, sensing his growing need for space as the piles of his past disappeared. I watched him from the kitchen window, putting aside his dinner, a triangular figure in a lawn chair silhouetted by the arching, pyrelike bonfire, its black plume blotting out the stars.

Oh, yeah, I knew about fires in this pit.

*　*　*

Scorching mad and with my jaw set, I pursed my lips and laid a small trap for Mr. Exterminator. "I've had a little trouble with yellow jackets," I said in the most helpless voice I could muster with a tiny overlay of Southern drawl. "But I know how to handle them. Just mix up a little napalm: some gasoline and laundry detergent. Pour it down the hole and light it."

The dismay spreading across his face was delightful. Mr. Exterminator took the bait. "Never do that," he reprimanded as if I were a child. "You don't know how dangerous it is. Don't ever try to handle this yourself. Call me."

"Oh, I don't think so," I said sweetly. "It's great fun. Fire in the hole, especially after dark."

I had actually quit doing Jim's style of fire-in-the-hole killing in favor of foaming spray insecticide, just as I had shifted over to Liquid Nails, but the wicked pleasure I got from baiting and shocking Mr. Exterminator was enough to keep me buoyant for the rest of the day, pleased I could play both my part and Jim's in screwing around with people's heads.

When we were young, Jim and I arrogantly likened ourselves to the twice-married-and-divorced Richard Burton and Elizabeth Taylor and their practiced hip-cat intellectualism of the '6os. Jim had Burton's glowering charm, and I could rant almost as well as Taylor, just not as shrieky. We loved them in the movie *Who's Afraid of Virginia Woolf?* for the complexity of the game they played. In their spirit, we played. Not very nice games, but interesting ones. Everyone plays these games on one level or another, and everyone keeps track, even though few would admit it. We kept track on our Personal Cruelties list, which was stored in the same drawer as the envelopes of signed bets. Nothing breaks up an escalating spat like pulling out a notebook to write down a transgression. *That's it, you've had it. I'm writing this down!* I hadn't written down anything since Jim died. He wasn't playing anymore.

But when he was alive, he was a patient, careful master of personal games. Jim delighted in convincing someone that he held a position that was opposite of something they held dear. Often we would tag-team to hide a snare in a conversation in order to challenge boasted ethics, politics, or mystical beliefs. Mostly it was Jim's game. I was the enabler, his foil. In his smooth, deep voice he'd play out a line. After a few back-and-forths, people would become enraged at his supposed racism, bigotry, sexism, xenophobia, or homophobia. Ironically, Jim usually didn't even have an opinion on the subject at hand; it just amused him to watch people sputter and fail to logically stand up for what they claimed they believed. But now I didn't need Jim. I could be both of us.

Except when it came to having a decent conversation. I had a bad Jim habit in that category. I'd been able to extinguish the demons in my office and triumph over the floods – my new gardens were struggling but holding promise – but I wasn't doing so well in keeping up both sides of a conversation or feeling like I even had a single decent thought.

A few weeks earlier, slumped deep into the cavernous oversize sofa chair in the lower level of the house, where I camped out wrapped in Jim's flannel shirt on Saturday nights, drifting in the wee hours watching movies, I'd been awakened to the dullness of my brain. Lila had been sleeping sprawled across me, belly side up, paws loose and floppy, breaking my rule of no dogs on the furniture. I was trying to meld psychically with the morose, indulgent characters of the movie, envious of how their rarified style of madness was so well suited to their smug intelligence. Their brains worked so well even under the weight of dysfunction. The movie, *Proof,* was almost over when frowning Catherine, the conflicted mathematical genius played by a pale and halting Gwyneth Paltrow, paused to consider how much time she wasted on the things that didn't really matter to her. Eating spaghetti in frustration instead of working on proving her mathematical proof. Waiting to inherit her father's insanity. Responding to and tending others instead of nurturing her own intellect.

I'd shoved over Lila and pulled myself up out of the depths of the chair to push aside the stack of mail-order DVDs next to the wine glass on the table, in search of the remote. "Get!" I'd yelled at Digs, who was sleeping at the foot of the chair. She gave me the sheepdog hard-eye and reluctantly moved. The remote was jammed into the cushion. I perched on the edge of the table-size ottoman and hit the back arrow. The credits reversed and Paltrow jerked backward in time until I got to the spot that had ejected me from the chair.

> How many days have I lost?
> How can I get back to the place where I started?
> I'm outside a house trying to find my way in.
> But it is locked.
> And the blinds are down.
> And I've lost the key.
> And I can't remember what the rooms look like

Or where I put anything.
And if I dare go in inside, I wonder . . .
Will I ever be able to find my way out?

I picked up a ballpoint pen and the wine-stained steno pad I kept beside the chair and backed up the DVD again and again, crossing out and rewriting until I got the lines right. Then I ripped the sheet out of the notebook and headed to my used-to-be-Jim's-bedroom office down the hallway. In the oasis of light at my desk, I opened my journal and stapled in the paper. Across the top in unsteady block printing I wrote A DEAD INTELLECT.

I had not had a good conversation since Jim died, not that I had any confidence I could hold up my end of one, but I couldn't shake off a gnawing jones for a dicey, confrontational, stimulating exchange about something weighty, such as the conflict between the static and the dynamic. That had been a good one a few years back. It had exploded while Jim and I were reading (together, but separately) Robert Pirsig's book *Lila: An Inquiry into Morals,* an unacclaimed follow-up to *Zen and the Art of Motorcycle Maintenance.*

We had been so struck by the power of the idea and how it operated everywhere. If things are too static, they die. If they are too dynamic, it's chaos. I even named Lila after the book. Surviving the dynamics of being put in a crate to drown, then the static of being shackled to a chain, and later the flux of the animal shelter – all in her puppyhood before me – gave her a keen awareness of how sliding up and down the static and dynamic scale could alter one's life.

Jim's copy of that book was mildewing in a box in the storage area above the workshop in the pole barn. Along with hundreds of others. The books would be ruined like the garden shed (just as I had warned Jim when he put them up there) if they spent one more damp winter unprotected.

On a hot Saturday morning in August, I rattled open the two high overhead garage doors and walked into the pole barn. Not a trace of breeze. A thin layer of moisture coated my skin, and I hadn't even started working yet. More air would be needed for book sorting.

I walked to the back of the building and undid the latches of the sliding rail door in the back wall and managed to shove the resistant twenty-five-foot door down its gummy track. Wiping the sweat from my forehead with the tail of my T-shirt, I looked up to the space above the workshop. Boxes and boxes of books ten feet up.

I knew this meant ladder work. Ladders make me nervous. Having fallen backward years ago, I couldn't climb a ladder without seeing the dreamlike, slow-motion drifting of the ladder away from the gutter followed by the sped-up crash into the yew bushes below.

A few feet away, the giant, orange fiberglass, construction-grade ladder loomed. I beckoned the inner warrior woman who had beaten the flood. She, and her buff muscles, wrestled the monster ladder over to the wall. I told her to get the angle right. Too steep and I would fall back. Too far and it would lose its grip and slide down. Then I took over, not trusting her. This would require nuance. I kicked at the swivel foot pads until they felt steady, flat, and gripping.

My mouth dry, patting the back pocket of my jeans to be sure I had my cell phone in case I survived a fall to the cement floor, I centered my cross-trainer in the first broad rung. The ladder felt stable. I looked up, took a deep breath, put my hands on the rungs in front of me, and began to methodically climb, leaning back a little as I went to see how much wiggle room I had. Carefully moving and testing, I shifted from rung to rung. At the top, I pushed against the ladder as I wrapped my leg around the tip of the extended rail and crawled onto the thick, muggy stillness above the workshop. The ladder held, sort of like Jim, steady and firm against my pressure.

I duckwalked under the steep rafters that angled sharply over the workshop attic to the clamped-on aluminum work light and switched it on. Boxes. Stacked two and three deep, all with Jim's tight, scratchy handwriting. *Vietnam novels, #1 of 5. Philosophy. Mystery. Science. S. I.*

magazines. I realized I didn't have a clear plan. Did I really want all of his Vietnam War novels? Did I want stacks of old magazines?

When I lifted the soft cardboard flaps of the nearest unmarked box, the tang of mildew and stale cigarette smoke tickled my nose. It was full of spiral-bound notebooks – his journals. I pulled out the one in front: 1998, the year his mother had died. I pulled one out toward the back: 1975, the year a bunch of us had gone to Alaska for adventure and to get rich working on the pipeline. I flipped it open. Terse one- and two-sentence entries about a trip to Arizona and Colorado with people I'd only heard of. Stopped in a bar here. Slept there. I turned a clump of pages. Now at Fort Wainwright in Fairbanks. Notes from his soil analysis classes with diagrams of the oil pipeline and facts about sand and silt. I sat back on my haunches. Jim had made me promise to burn these journals; I was going to have to read them first. This box was headed for the house.

The next box, unmarked, held a set of numbered notebooks. It was the Vietnam novel he'd written in the '70s but never showed to me, "The Sucker's Punch." Three-hundred-and-seventy-pages written in hard-pressed, dark pencil across seven spiral notebooks. There were also stacks of college essays. I picked up a pack of index cards rubber-banded together. *Realism, Idealism, Skepticism* . . . his handy reference system to the theories of philosophy over the ages.

People who didn't know Jim would draw back a little when I told them he worked in a factory. The immediate, silent judgment that he was somehow less. But I never knew anyone who could hold a candle to the purity of his personal curiosity and study not only of philosophy but also of religion, psychology, history, and science. Systematic and careful with index cards and notebooks. He didn't do it for a job or for accolades. He did it for himself.

I closed the box and scooted it over to the ladder. Wiping away the salty sweat stinging my eyes, I surveyed the stacks of remaining boxes.

"What did you have in mind here, Jim?" I asked the rafters. "How am I supposed to get all of these boxes down?" I stood on the edge of the workshop roof – the only place with enough room for me to stand up straight – and hoisted up a box, quickly moving my hand under its mushy bottom. It was pretty heavy, but not too heavy. There was no way to hold both the box and the rungs; there wasn't enough room for the big box between the front of me and the ladder. I would have to walk down face out, leaning my back against the ladder. Not OSHA-approved, I was sure.

Unable to see my feet under the box, I sucked in my breath and swung my left leg over the rail. Feeling around with my foot and finding the rung, I slid in the heel of my shoe and shifted my weight to it. Then I brought my right foot over and faced the empty space in front of an unanchored me.

I looked down. The dogs sat at the base of the ladder. Diggity, tail wagging and eyes bright, thought a good game might be afoot. Lila, shoulders hunched, whites of her eyes showing, braced herself for the worst. The box grew heavier; its sides seemed more like fabric than cardboard, the seams threatening to give. I didn't have time to tarry. I moved down the ladder. Careful concentration. Step, step, step. Then the security of the concrete floor. I set the box down and felt my buzz powering up. I could do this.

Over and over I walked the boxes of books down, each time knowing that a mistake would land me smashed on the floor. I was not anywhere near as careful with the boxes packed with magazines. "Why did you keep magazines?" I scolded dead Jim. Those boxes I dropped from the attic to the floor in satisfyingly soft explosions that grew into a slippery, spreading mound of *Skeptical Inquirer* (Jim had every issue except the first one), *Science News, Psychology Today,* and *Discover.*

* * *

I tossed an empty Rolling Rock beer bottle into a used plastic paint bucket, belched loudly, and eased into the aluminum lawn chair, hoping not to break through its frayed blue and white webbing. The drone of cicadas throbbed in the surrounding dark pastures, and the tease of a cool night breeze drifted in through the open doors. Above me in the rafters, moths beat against the blazing lights and hungry bats darted after.

Shoulder-high towers of books filled the back half of the barn, sorted by topic. On the shelves that used to hold Jim's inventions were more books, ones I didn't think I wanted. I was thankful that Jim had cleared them out. Inconveniently in the middle was a small, slumping mountain of magazines. To one side was a pile of broken, flabby boxes. The dogs were sprawled out sleeping on the cool concrete floor. The workshop attic was empty.

I ran my eyes down the titles of the books in the stack closest to me, stopping at Edward O. Wilson's *Consilience: The Unity of Knowledge*. Groaning, my back aching, and my legs wobbly, I stood to unstack the books to get to it. With a sigh I sat back down, running my hands over its smooth black cover. I had a feeling I was looking for something. It was another book Jim and I had read (together, but separately). It was about how knowledge could be more powerful if people would simply agree to use the same basic methods to compile data. My marked copy was inside the house. I opened the deckle-edged pages to a passage Jim had noted with vertical pencil marks in the margin: "Without the stimulus and guidance of emotion, rational thought slows and disintegrates."

I hugged the open book tight against my chest, tears coming to my eyes. I was obsessed with Jim in a way I never had been when he was alive. I couldn't have a thought without Jim in it. Think of a mountain, see Jim. Think of the ocean, Jim was there. Go for a walk, Jim went too. Touch anything, and Jim was there. But I didn't remember why Jim had marked this sentence among pithy sentences.

Because I wasn't him.

Only Jim could be Jim. I could be only me. I couldn't be both of us.

We weren't of one mind when he was alive. And we couldn't be of one mind now that he was dead. But he had formed a side of me. The intersection of us. And it had collapsed at his death. Like an adjoining wall between two buildings, gone. Not all of me was destroyed, just this section. This place that I used to push against and be pushed back. A place that was distinctly not me. Now vacant.

We become fixed in who we are. Fight as we may or may not against the static, most of our lives we are boxed in by obligation, fear, or habit. This vacancy was an opening, like a garden space opened by a storm forcing shade to sunny and boggy to dry.

Zoom out from the narrow, and you can see that the hosta garden was once lawn, once pasture, once locust grove, once oak forest, once bog, once glacial ice, once shallow sea. Land doesn't care what it was or is.

But I cared who I was. And this understanding of what lay before me was like the air that stirs around the wings of a yellow swallowtail butterfly paused on a fuchsia zinnia bloom.

I put Jim's book back in my lap and flipped to a new page: "The legacy of the Enlightenment is the belief that entirely on our own we can know, and in knowing, understand, and in understanding, choose wisely." It seemed a good point. I didn't have a single idea what to do with the now-open side of me I had shared with Jim, but I could, on my own, choose wisely.

9

Balancing Concentrate

"Momma, just relax," Emily instructed me over the phone. "There's no reason to get all stressed out. I'll be there on Sunday night. On Monday we'll get up, have coffee, go into town, get massages, and have lunch."

"Massages? Lunch?"

"Yes, I booked massages for us. To set the tone for the week. Let's just have fun."

I tapped my mechanical pencil on my calendar in displaced irritation. The week I'd taken off work was blocked off with her name written across the days. "That leaves us just four days to do everything. Your wedding is Saturday."

"You think I don't know that? Chill out; everything will be fine."

Monday morning found us in a row of plastic chairs by metal lockers in the backroom maze of a hair salon.

"This isn't very spa-like," I said to Emily, pointing to a dirty spot on my terry-cloth robe. "They need to wash these between customers. Aren't we supposed to be lounging in bamboo chairs next to a gurgling fountain, not in a locker room?"

"You need a massage worse than I do." Emily smiled sweetly and patted my hand as if I were the nervous bride. "You can't expect too much. It's a hair salon. The massages are part of my bridal package."

She was right. The hospital-style plastic chairs had triggered the image of Jim's last look. I was sick, sick, sick of having his last look pop up wherever I went, but it still came anyway, like an unwanted dog that followed me everywhere.

"Did I tell you that I took a breathing workshop to help me remember how to breathe again?"

Emily looked at me and blinked her eyes, unsure how to respond. I guessed my out-of-place comment made her hold her breath.

She was saved from me when a young woman with blond-streaked hair and penciled-in arched eyebrows called Emily's name. She gratefully scuttled off.

I've always had trouble with shallow breathing, ironic for one who had to coach Jim on how to take his last breaths. I think I learned to hold my breath at critical moments as a child, standing at attention in the living room while being lectured by my father about how I should improve upon my errant ways. Holding my breath protected me somehow. It took me out of the room but with enough consciousness to say, "Yes, sir," at the right time. Anxiety levels were high in our house during my teen years; my father was slowing dying from cancer, and I was a difficult, rebellious kid.

I had done a little deep breathing during my free-spirited hippie years but started holding my breath again when I went back to college in my late twenties and kept holding it. This mild asphyxiation was pointed out to me by a business coach I once hired to get me to relax at work. "When you run meetings, when things are important, you don't breathe deeply. This makes everyone nervous. If you would breathe easily, everyone would relax and be more open to new ideas," she'd told me while introducing me to my diaphragm.

After Jim died I had lost my breath again to the buzz. I liked the buzz. It got things done. It protected me and made me strong. But it sucked air from the space around me to fuel its combustion. Yet as the last suffocatingly hot and humid days of summer had relaxed into the coolness of October, as the hazy skies turned clear blue and the leaves of the sugar maples tipped with yellow and then flushed fluorescent red-orange, the buzz ran out of juice.

But I still wasn't breathing. It was like I had root rot, submerged too long in memories and unable to uptake oxygen. I knew how to breathe well – *inhale slowly, count to five, exhale slowly while counting to eight* – but had a hard time remembering to do it. I felt off center. That's why I took the breathing workshop. To get a shove back toward center.

I didn't feel centered when I slid my face into the towel-covered cradle of the salon massage table in a tiny room, and I suspected that my massage therapist also had a color job sitting in foils while she ran in to lightly run inexperienced fingers over my muscles. I really did need a massage, but I wasn't going to get one here.

Through the thin walls I could hear Emily's voice bubbling. She wasn't talking about her future husband; she was talking about her dog, Chief, a white shepherd. He was going to come down the aisle in a black bowtie with the ring bearer.

Jim's last look faded away for a time. I synchronized my breathing to the rhythm of the shallow kneading on the surface of my back. *Inhale slowly, count to five, exhale slowly while counting to eight. It will be fine,* I chanted to myself.

A half hour later, reeking of sandalwood oil, I walked into the salon reception area to find Emily making final arrangements for Saturday morning, when bride and bridesmaids would fill every seat in the salon, getting hair piled and curled, fingers and toes painted the same shade of purple. Waiting for her to finish, I absently played with the tubes of lotions and bottles of iridescent nail polish on the counter. A display of narrow indigo glass bottles caught my eye.

"It's an oil, a balancing concentrate," said the receptionist, unscrewing the lid to a sample bottle. "Try it. Roll it on your temple. It dissolves tension."

I ran the miniature roller ball first on one and then on the other temple. It tingled and the scent of peppermint and chamomile floated in the air around my face.

"I'm getting it," I said smiling. "Two bottles. One for Emily and one for me."

* * *

When we got home, I cleared off the old oak dining room table. "Wedding Central," I said, getting out my copy of the *Martha Stewart Wedding Workbook,* which was chock-full of checklists for everything from creating a budget to signing up for dance lessons. "Do you have your copy? Did you do the worksheets I gave you?"

"No, I made my own book," said Emily as she extracted a bulging binder from a big blue modern-art tote bag. "See, I've been collecting ideas." She flipped open the binder to the Flowers tab and waved her hand over photographs cut from magazines – styles of wedding arbor swags, cascading planter flower combinations, compact hand-tied calla lily and freesia nosegays, flower-girl baskets, curvy bouton-nieres, and dried-flower table bouquets. "We'll combine the look of this with these flowers in urns like that," she said, pointing here and there. "I have the urns and containers in my car."

She turned and pulled out a set of small metal vases from her bag. She fitted the pointed ends of one vase into a little matching stand. "These are tussy-mussies," she said.

"Tussy-mussies?" I giggled.

"You use the vase to make a bridesmaid bouquet instead of nose-gays in tape and wire," she said. "The vase is really a handle for the bridesmaids to hold. After the ceremony, the vase sits in its own stand and makes a table decoration for the wedding party table. We'll use purple and white Peruvian lilies in these. I'll carry purple calla lilies. I have the flowers ordered from Kroger. We can pick them up the night before the wedding."

"Do you have a to-do list?" I asked, wondering what else she had in her bag.

"Let's make one now," she said, opening her binder to an empty page.

Two pages long. Six single different cakes instead of one big one, plus a cheesecake decorated like a baseball for the groom. Meet the harpist on campus at the university's school of music to choose what she would play. Do the song list for the DJ. Push little silver dragonflies into a few hundred candles. Bouquets. Planters. Wedding arch. Corsages. Make a seating chart. Fill small net bags with lavender for guests to throw instead of rice. Make earrings for the bridesmaids. Find a silver tray for guests to engrave their names into. Write, design, and print programs. Finish making the wedding rings – Emily had been working on them for months.

All of this in four days.

At least we'd decided to get a caterer instead of having the wedding at my house. I got our bottles of balancing concentrate out of the plastic bag from the salon.

But Emily's list was short one important item: hang out with friends. Each day Emily would do a few things. Her cell phone would ring, she'd fall into an excited conversation, and then say, "I'm going into town to hang out. Don't worry, we'll be fine. While I'm gone could you [fill in the blank]?"

Each night we scratched off a few "done" things from the list. Each morning we decided on what really didn't need to be done and rolled on dabs of balancing concentrate.

"If we don't get it done, no one will know we meant to do it," Emily said, shooing away my tense urge to pick up our pace. "Who cares if there's a seating chart? Besides, who are we to decide where our friends sit? They can figure that out."

But people did expect cake, and we were making the cakes ourselves to save money. Emily had very specific plans for a collection of different cakes, all with a smooth chocolate ganache icing that would sit on staggered silver stands. Repeatedly I had urged Emily to do a test run, but she'd put me off. At three o'clock on Thursday morning, I silently said *I told you so* to the kitchen cabinets. Four cakes with seized lumpy icing were in the trash, and Emily was on an hour-long trip to town to buy cake mix.

Emily's list was more undone than done, and in a few hours, just about the time we should be finished with the second batch of cakes, I would be sleeplessly greeting the new in-laws, people I hardly knew. Emily was moving to her motel honeymoon suite, and they were moving in downstairs for three nights. The downstairs bathroom remodel was still incomplete after six months, waiting for a back-ordered shower door. The pressure was on.

By late Friday afternoon, Emily's list was useless, we were so behind. It was just a couple hours before the rehearsal pizza and beer party. I was in jeans in the garage, surrounded by four huge urns and two massive bouquets in tall silver vases. Plumes of silver maiden grass, tall stalks of dangling dark-wine pokeweed berries, green-and-white trailing vinca, and branches of pink-tinged white hydrangea blossoms filled a half dozen white plastic paint pails. The dogs were eyeing the whole mess suspiciously, sniffing the growing piles of discarded stem ends and leaves, and picking up on my frantic state.

Instead of a fancy dinner, we were enslaving relatives to decorate the reception hall. Emily and the in-laws had already left with the dried flowers, candles, and vases for the tables. The groom was on his way to the hall from Indianapolis, and my brother and sister would arrive with spouses at any moment.

Around the edges of the white urns little white, airy flowers floated above the dainty olive and purple leaves of the Tahitian bridal-veil plants that were intertwined with the pink, tri-cornered blossoms and trailing deep purple leaves of wandering Jew. All that was left to do was to finish making three-foot arching bouquets in the center of the urns.

I put down my yellow-handled florist knife, took off the dirty garden gloves, and briefly admired my unchipped purple fingernail polish. The urns were looking good – glorious, in fact. Now if I could just get finished with them. Rubbing my aching back, I wished for a little buzz to call forth some overlooked ounce of creativity from my exhausted being.

I had stepped back to consider the vases, the urns, and the buckets of flowers when the crunch of thick stems under my feet brought me up short. That familiar sound. The released scent of fresh. The wires on the table. The green floral foam soaking in a galvanized bucket. The knife with a sheepsfoot pruner blade. I was standing in a tiny, rough version of my family's Indianapolis flower shop of forty years ago.

* * *

My family had a series of stores up until shortly after I graduated from high school, and the whole family had worked in the stores, including my brother's wife. Mostly the bouquets were done by floral designers we hired, which was a good thing, since I was never able to win even a junior florist design contest. Daddy was the sales guy and merchandiser. Mother was the accountant and corsage maker. As a toddler, my first job was sweeping stem ends and discarded flowers. Older, I rode shotgun in the step van, jumping out and scouting the graves as my brother drove slowly through winding cemetery roads to deliver Memorial Day baskets of red geraniums and pink petunias to place by headstones – before the days of plastic flowers. Later I moved on to making piles of tufts for corsages, each one a task of looping wire over a rectangle of pastel nylon net and then twisting the wire into little tails. Whole Saturdays were given over to the dull chore of taking inventory or cleaning the store's big sandstone patio and showroom and dusting the glass shelves filled with glazed pots, colored-glass bud vases, and big-skirted china ladies with space in the back for plants or a bouquet. For us, Christmas started in July and ended in a tired slump on Christmas Eve after making hundreds of bows and wreaths.

I hated working in the shop and couldn't wait to have a boss who wasn't also a parent, but I loved the details of the store. The fragrant cool humidity, complex sweetness, and tropical color behind the thick-walled, heavy-handled door of our walk-in "Refrigerated Display Room." The milk glass vases with pink tea roses and dainty baby's breath. The impossibly brilliant blue and orange spikes of bird of paradise flowers. Pails of aromatic eucalyptus. Frecklelipped, fleshy purple and cream cymbidium orchids. Long-stemmed roses – ruby red, Texas yellow, and snow-white kissed with pink. Fivegallon buckets packed with blazing yellow mums, bushy leather ferns, and hardy boxwood.

The boxes of wired net tufts, rhinestones, and pearls that my patient grandmother made by the hundreds. The pungent black dirt in the potting area. The big, deep concrete sinks. The cavernous garage shared with the neighboring hardware store. Hot wax dripped onto the backs of Fuji mums to keep the spidery petals from falling. Heavy rosebuds pierced with thick wire wrapped tightly around stems and covered with sticky green florist tape. Spools of satin ribbon hanging from a metal rod, some pastel and narrow, others wide and bold. And the crunch of the ankle-deep stems thick under foot.

* * *

The sharp alarm barking of the dogs brought me up short and broke the spell. I shoved them out and opened the overhead door to greet my brother's white sedan. He and his wife, along with my West Coast sister and her husband, emerged, all four doors opening simultaneously. Smiles faded into quizzical looks as they saw the floral disarray in the garage.

"It's the last-minute-bouquet crazies," I explained, gesturing palms up. "There's been too much to do and not enough time." I knew my state of unpreparedness fed right into my family status as the never-quite-together little sister.

My brother's wife, the reigning family queen of being tidy and on time, clucked good-naturedly at my lateness and then asked, "What can I do?"

"Give bouquet advice," I said, privately stinging with insufficiency for being late and undone. "This center arrangement, does it need more grass plumes? Is this stalk of poke too high? Where should I add these puffy white tulle bows?"

Hand on the hip of her slim, stylish trousers, she cast an evaluating florist eye. "Move the poke to the right to add more purple there. You need lots more grass plumes. Do you have them?"

"Point me in the right direction; I'll go get some," said my sister as she kissed me. "I have my boots on." She held up one foot to show off her fancy cowgirl boots.

I pointed to the maidenhair grass plumes and handed her a knife. "Go cut more of this. Don't worry about the dogs. Just walk out there like you own the place, and they'll quit barking. Get some sea oats too – over by the fence – and watch out for the dog poop."

Her husband looked on as if he had been transported to another planet populated by crazy florists as my brother reverted into delivery organization mode.

It all came together, but I was nervous. I wanted to feel relieved that the family saved me, but instead I was ashamed. Almost sixty years old and still trailing behind. With dog poop in the yard.

Cringing inside, I led our caravan of cars to the reception hall in town, more than once miscalculating and stranding my family on the other side of red lights.

The next day the sky was a clear and vivid azure blue. The sugar maples surrounding the pond and log cabin, where the finished-at-the-last-moment wedding arch stood, were a perfect deep gold in the brilliant afternoon sunlight. A nippy breeze flirted with the grass plumes in the planters.

Horse carriage, harp, I do, rings, purple signature cocktails, roasted tenderloin, the slicing of the cake-mix cakes with decent ganache icing, and couple toasting flashed by as if in a distant dream with its own sound track starting with Bach and devolving over the hours into Chuck Berry. Alone at the table with wadded white linen napkins at soiled place settings, I poured another glass of special mother-of-the-bride champagne, briefly studying the loose, wrinkly skin of my hand and growing collection of age spots. The white calla lilies in my wrist corsage canted to one side. I pulled it off and tossed it on the table. Mother would be disgusted if she could see this sloppy corsage work; too bad I hadn't paid more attention when she was teaching me.

I scooted the padded party chair around so that I could look across the darkened room, tugging at the hem of my black and purple velvet dress that was much too short for the mother of the bride. At tables encircling the dance floor gossiping clumps of friends and relatives (including those who had tried to force me to catch the bridal bouquet) sat with heads nodding like patches of multicolored spring columbines.

It would be a long time before spring, and I sensed a deepening of roots among the crowd as they prepared to hunker down for the coming winter. The wedding was like a renewal of the hearth and the gathering of things that keep heart and soul together for the cold days ahead. Emily was on the dance floor, hot, I was sure, in her long white dress and feet surely blistered, committed now to a future that had little to do with me. If I'd been a good mother, I would have been weepy-eyed and sentimental, but she was thirty-five and had married her live-in boyfriend of ten years. I wasn't even sure why they were getting married, except to acquiesce to convention. They weren't even planning on having children. "If we get the urge to have children, we'll get a boat," the groom had once said to me. Maybe she was marrying him for health insurance. It didn't seem much of a change, except for the hole in my bank account that had paid for this nice padded chair I was sitting on and my bottle of exceptional champagne.

I poured a little more of it into my glass flute and watched the pale froth build and then flatten and the tiny lines of bubbles break at the surface. It was impossible not to imagine Jim here next to me, and I couldn't help but be glad he wasn't. He hated parties, crowds, and dancing. I remembered that last year he had even asked if he had to go to Emily's wedding. It was great not having to nursemaid Jim's panicky angst or to apologize for his surly antisocial muteness.

I drained my glass, put my heels back on, and stood to find a wobbly champagne balance. It was time to dance. Free-form hippie-chick style, the kind of dancing that embarrasses you later if you think about it, so you don't.

Dancing by myself. It was not a new thing. Not once in the thirty-one years I knew him did Jim ever dance in public with me. At Rum Point Beach on the island of Grand Cayman, a full moon hanging over the Caribbean Sea, he got pissed because I danced with an islander to the reggae band. In a narrow, packed New Orleans bar where an accordion, fiddle, and washboard Cajun band was pumping out the most infectious riffs, Jim paid a disgusting guy ten dollars to dance with me. On a weekend excursion with friends to Madison, Indiana, down by the Ohio River, the Bigger Than Elvis band played fine retro at the Electric Lady bar, and Jim refused to dance with me but did with my friend.

Well, he wasn't here. Not here to get pissed. Not here to screw with me. Not here to not dance with me.

Slipping into the circle of young dancers modestly shaking their shoulders and shuffling foot to foot, I swung my hip into the dirty little secret that I was glad Jim wasn't there. Thrust my shoulder into all my little sister insecurities. Snapped my fingers at the vacant, collapsed side of me that I had yet to understand. Swung into all the whispers of the reception crowd about me dancing alone in my too-short dress. Outside, a cold rain was coming from the west on the back of a chilly wind.

10

Swoop

I stared at the willow basket filled with oversized fiber and wood balls on my young boss's credenza. It was a safe, nondescript place to rest my eyes during the most horrible performance review of my life, worse than the one I'd had the previous February just days before Jim died.

"It's not that you don't know marketing," she said as I continued to avoid making eye contact with her. "You probably know it better than anyone on the team. You could probably write a book on it, and maybe you should." She cleared her throat, and I stirred myself to look up. "It's just that you don't fit into our culture. I can't put my finger on it, but for whatever reason, people just aren't comfortable working around you. They feel intimidated. Truthfully, I really enjoy the work we do together, but the team – it's just not working. And we're a team here. We have to fit together. You'd probably be better in upper management, but there are no positions there."

Since going back to work, I'd had all the symptoms of a daylily with root-knot nematodes, a disease that strikes field plants transplanted to the suburbs – a loss of vigor, slow deterioration, poor growth, a yellow cast, and wilting. The best option in this situation is to choose plants that are not susceptible to this disease. And just two weeks shy of the one-year anniversary of Jim's death, I was being uprooted for better stock. I had to admit, my young boss was right.

I had forced myself to return to my job a month after Jim died. I'd felt nauseous about it, hunting again and again in my finances for some unfound confirmation that I didn't need the money. My financial counselor told me to hang on to the job no matter what, to get the pension, and bank as much of my pay as I could. So I had gone back, driving the 150-mile round trip daily to the northern suburbs of Indianapolis.

My boss shuffled the papers in front of her as she listed my failings. "I have to cover for you. You get into trouble politically. You just haven't lived up to expectations. You haven't shown the kind of leadership we need. You have a rogue agenda." She paused; her hand flitted across her mouth. "I don't know why you've done so poorly. As far as I can see, you never had any grief over Jim's death; your relationship was just a marriage of convenience anyway."

I shifted in my chair, stunned by her arrogance, as if she was the arbitrator of how I was supposed to love or grieve, of the right or wrong ways to do it. I had told her about getting married for insurance, about enjoying our independence. Now she had twisted that into a hardhearted dismissal. My inability to think clearly, the buzzing, was not enough. She'd wanted an obvious display.

My mind drifted to the day I'd gone back to work the year before. Opening the laptop. Forcing my finger to hit the power button. My head heavy on my desk in my arms. Then the weeks that followed when I would leave meetings to hide a crying spell I felt on its way. Jim's last look floating in front of me while people prattled on about how to reinvent the basic marketing plan format. I had asked my doctor for something to make me quit crying. She'd prescribed a fancy antidepressant that made me not care if I made it to work or even out of bed.

I quit the pills and just sucked it up. I put on a smile and came to work. The bootstrap method, the one taught in my family, that's what worked for me. I'm a woman who made my way up during the eighties and nineties; to me it isn't professional to bring your personal life to work. My grief wasn't for public consumption anyway. It wasn't performance art, put on for people who wanted to examine and lap up the sticky sap that oozed from my wounds.

Sharing is not my style anyway. I hate the smarmy word *share*. I would like to *share* with you blah, blah, blah – makes me sick. And I'm not good at working with women who want to get personal and discuss things to death. I want to focus on the work, set breakthrough strategies, and get things done.

Then I noticed she was still talking.

"It's nothing personal. We're making changes in the department. Your job is being eliminated in a few months, but we're offering you a different position. It would be a demotion."

Maybe some truth telling on my part would work, some emotion maybe. "You know," I said as I scooted back my chair, "my time here has been so slow that it seems granular. My feet feel like lead weights. I am glug, glugging down in deep water while the person I used to be is a small, diminishing light far away above the surface."

She seemed mildly pleased and pushed some documents across the desk toward me, pointing to paragraphs and reading upside down. There was a dull ringing in my ears. I fought its dampening; I had to negotiate some kind of exit deal. As I struggled to keep my face neutral, my mind drifted. Why was it so hard to pay attention? I remembered an article about how emotional states can facilitate or hamper the processing of information. If people are in positive states of mind, they can cope with threatening information, like the diagnosis of cancer, and make good decisions. But if they are not, they make suboptimal decisions that make them feel better right away but screw them in the long run. I needed to make a good long-term decision here.

The tickle of little neurons scrambling together in my brain, the last brave remnants of cognitive thought, brought me to consciousness again as my boss leaned across her desk. "So is this a surprise for you?"

I ignored her, signed something, picked up the rest of the papers, and said, "Let me read over everything, and I'll get back to you."

She shook my hand and smiled with hooded eyes. "That's okay; really, I should thank you for being so understanding."

Now everything was really undone. Both Jim and my career were dead.

Winding down the beige hallway maze, focused on how carpet patterns are designed to hide the load of traffic and coffee spills, I experimented with my posture until I achieved a nice, straight feeling – unhunched shoulders, head high and balanced perfectly over my spine, like a dancer. Faces turned and bobbed up as I passed the open doorway of a conference room. I wondered if they all knew. How many of them had made secret visits to complain about me? I imagined my boss over in the human resources department plotting this terrible day, discussing tactics.

I slunk into my office and closed the door. Outside my window a heavy bank of clouds hung over the interstate highway. A big February blizzard was forecast, and the snow had already started. I stuffed the performance review papers in my briefcase, sent an email asking to take the next day off, and slipped on my coat without waiting for approval. I welcomed its snug softness around me. Wet, thick snowflakes splatted down from the sky as I whipped out of the parking lot.

My mind, a latent live coal in what I had thought were cold ashes, began to ignite. The redness spread, synapses sparking and arcing across corroded connections – burning, boiling, cringing, outraged, aghast. I put a smooth-gloved finger on my twitching lower right eyelid to calm it.

Veering away from more caffeine, I bypassed Starbucks. *Oh, just to get home. Get out of these heels, put on jeans. Have a glass of wine, some of that Malbec, or maybe a gin and tonic, or maybe both. Make a nice dinner. Think. Read the small print.*

Traffic was already bogged down. By the time I turned off I-465 onto the state road south, icy clumps of wet snow held the windshield wipers up in the air. I pulled over to clean them and stepped into the deep, dirty slush at the side of the highway, the fine leather of my shoes forever ruined. A van slid at an angle, missing me.

I drove on, a death grip on the steering wheel, past cars scattered like toys on the sides of the road. A steady, forward momentum through seventy-five miles of slick. The gas gauge ticked downward as the line of commuters crawled behind snowplows up the hills that led home. Four hours later I hit the garage door opener and pulled into the safe and dry space. That buzzy, cold emptiness inside me had been replaced with a hot, purposeful rage.

*   *   *

The next morning, light stretched across the new green kitchen counters highlighting the circle of sticky goo where the gin and tonic had been. My eye was twitching nervously. My head was thick from a restless night. Coffee. I needed coffee, but it would have to be half-caf to help control the twitch. A disturbing gurgle percolated in my gut.

With my jaw clenched, I took the coffee to the bathroom and sighed heavily in the mirror as I set the blue pottery mug on the vanity top. A combative, cruddy-and-twitchy-eyed me looked back. I put my finger on my eyelid and examined the accursed vertical wrinkles above my lip. I stuck my face under the faucet to wash the tension off and the crustiness from my eyes. Pulling in a long breath, I repeated the mantra from my new yoga DVD: *Relax the corners of your eyes, relax your temples, relax the surface of your face. With soft eyes look up.* A dab of cool cucumber-lily moisturizing lotion. Maybe my face did relax.

"Clarity of mind needs clarity of body," I thought as I popped a bran muffin from the batch of perfect ones I'd made over the weekend into the toaster oven. Cirrus sat politely on the empty stool next to me, tail curled neatly around her feet, front paws primly tucked side by side, watching me as I peeled a tiny, bright-orange tangerine. I coiled the leathery rind around my fingers and the idea of quitting my job around my mind.

We had paid off the house before Jim died, thanks to him. He paid off both of our halves of the mortgage from money he had inherited from his aunt. After his brain surgery he'd insisted on a new refrigerator, washer, and dryer and refused to let me pay half for any of it. He also had bought new flooring for the kitchen and dining room; tearing out blue Berber carpet and installing it was our last project together. "If the two of us, the addle-brained and the brain-damaged, can do this, anyone can," we'd laughed.

And he changed his will. "How could I have gotten through this without you?" he'd said as he asked me to call the attorney for an appointment. "You've sacrificed for me, so instead of my sister getting everything, I'm dividing it between the two of you. Naming you executor."

This was a reversal. When we had married so that I could be on his life insurance policy, we had signed an agreement to relinquish all spousal financial rights. Our laissez-faire relationship was never about money, or family building, until it reached this point. "I would rather that you stay alive," I'd said. I should have said thank you, but it seemed greedy at the moment, as if I wanted his money instead of him.

"My half of this house goes to you and my half of the family house goes to my sister," Jim had said with a wicked smile. "But I'm thinking about switching that so that the two of you will have to deal with each other. It would be a good joke."

I'd had to tread carefully. The smallest rise from me and he would have done it as a posthumous tease, and I absolutely did not want to be financially entangled with his sister. So I deflected and said again, "I would rather have you alive."

He grew serious. "If I die, this will help you be free."

Even after a year his estate was still not settled, but it would be soon. I had the precious, low-premium health insurance. Instead of allowing me to quit and go on vacation with Jim, it would allow me to take a chance with my employment. And I had a respectable veteran widow's pension ("Don't forget to go to the VA office after I croak," Jim had said, and, surprise, there was a lifetime pension for me, thanks to Agent Orange). I'd carefully parceled out his life insurance money to pay off my truck, fix the drainage, remodel the lower level, get not-yellow kitchen counters, and subsidize Emily's wedding. I didn't owe any money for anything.

It was time to ignore my financial counselor's advice to stick with the job for the pension and take Jim up on his offer of freedom. I could survive with a job running the cash register at the pizza joint halfway into town, especially if I didn't have to fill up the gas tank every other day. Maybe I would get chickens and become a self-sufficient farmer. I was close to that already. The closet under the stairs was packed with Ball jars gleaming with tomatoes, apple jelly, cucumber relish, green beans, and applesauce. The freezer was over-full with corn, blueberries, peppers, and grated zucchini. I could survive.

Plans for a moveable chicken coop spun through my head for a few minutes until I remembered Corvus, the young crow Jim had kept years ago. All the chairs and bookcases in Jim's study had to be covered with plastic sheeting due to the prodigious amount of bird shit, just from one smaller-than-a-chicken bird. A coop that I could move over the pasture would not eliminate poop on nest boxes and roosts. Not to mention frequent feedings, egg gathering, feather plucking, head chopping, and fending off coyotes. It would be cheaper and easier to buy a dozen eggs and pre-plucked chicken at the store. Screw being a farmer; I could sell the house and move into the art and flair of town. Start walking instead of driving. Get a bike. Make some new friends. I could go into town to the coffeehouse right now and get some mocha – sit at the wooden table next to the bookshelf, warm my hands on the white porcelain cup, run my finger along the loop of its handle, dip the tiny spoon into the chocolate swirled into the steamed milk.

I opened the wall of drapes that covered the expanse of windows across the upstairs living room. The dazzle of reflected snow flooded the room. A smooth plain of sparkling white snow stretched from the house and across the horse pastures, broken by the plowed road that bisected the view and the mountain of ice and sand piled at the end of my driveway. I wasn't going anywhere yet.

Deciding to quit my job and actually doing it were two different things. Like a dog turning around and around to lie down, I circled the idea. First letting it simmer while I chopped carrots and celery for a pot of chicken noodle soup. Then letting it seep into certainty while I wrote a script to follow. I wanted to do this right and didn't trust my angry mouth. The clock ticked late into the afternoon before I picked up the cordless phone.

"There's no point in throwing good after bad," I read from the script in my notebook. "Next Wednesday is my last day. I'll work from home between now and then. All my work is organized. It won't take long to write up a task list."

"I don't want it to look like you were fired," said my boss, guile slick under her words.

I didn't say, "Are you fucking kidding me? Is office politics all you think about?" Instead, I said, "Let's just tell people that I can't stand the commute," which was true.

It took me two days, more than eight hours altogether, to shovel out the driveway. And then I headed my Element to Indianapolis, task list already completed, to box up my stuff and sign paperwork.

When I walked to my office, past the glances, I knew that everyone knew. And that everyone knew that it wasn't because I hated the commute. I gathered the few books and files, put my spider plant in a box, and wrapped up photos and desk knickknacks. The crystal dinosaur I kept to remind myself to never stop learning or fall behind. The strip of photo booth pictures of Jim and me, with me kissing the cheek of a content, eyes-closed Jim in the last frame. And a small cherry frame that held a quote copied in a loopy open script. Long ago, back when people still wrote letters in longhand, a friend had sent it my way. I had carried it from job to job.

> Life is a long Dardanelles, My Dear Madam, the shores whereof are bright with flowers, which we want to pluck, but the bank is too high; & so we float on & on, hoping to come to a landing place at last – but swoop! We launch into the great sea! Yet the geographers say, even then we must not despair, because across the great sea, however desolate and vacant it may look, lie all Persia & the delicious lands round-about Damascus.
> – from Herman Melville in a letter to Hawthorne's wife, Sophia

I walked one last time down the beige hallway to my boss's office to let her know I was finished. Her door was ajar, and I knocked while walking in.

"I'm leaving. Here's my list of projects, what I will get done by Wednesday, and what will be left to do."

She gestured me to her chair. I did not want to sit, but I did.

"You can't quit," she said. "There's no one to do your work. No time. No talent. Would you consider a contract, or staying on until the spring?"

What's this? I thought I was a disaster. Suddenly I'm valuable? At least in the short term. Something had gone on behind the scenes, and as usual in this job I didn't know what, but I felt the fulcrum of power shift my way. "Let's make it simple. No contract. I stay in my job. No thirty-day performance evaluation. You don't turn in the bad review."

"Okay," she said, clearly ahead of me. "I'll give a standard review with a two percent raise. Your job will expire in May."

"And I quit coming to staff meetings," I said, charging ahead brazenly. "I work from home, not here."

"Deal." She scooted new papers for me to sign across her desk. "You have to agree not to sue for age discrimination. You'll get six month's severance pay too. Maybe there will be freelance work after this."

A spreadsheet opened up in my head, and numbers slotted themselves into rows and columns over the months ahead. I threw my signature across the pages, shook her hand, and left to go buy a case of cheap wine at Trader Joe's to store in the closet under the steps with the jars of tomatoes. Another snowstorm was forecast for the next day. This time I wasn't going to shovel the driveway. I would wait for it to melt.

11

The In Between

Jim and I were driving by an old railroad station converted into an antique shop. I wanted to stop. He didn't. I insisted. Once I got inside I remembered that I lived in the shop and had been rearranging all the antiques. I wanted to go down the path that I knew was out back. It was a smooth concrete walkway that wound through twisted, aromatic red cedars and beautiful boulders. Jim said no, he didn't want to go, he'd already been. I went without him, running dangerously fast, or maybe I was on a bicycle. Judges sitting at a table awaited me at the base of the hill. They showed me my new house and congratulated me on writing my book. One judge said he was my coach. He held out a red jacket with gold tassels, saying it was my reward, but I couldn't put it on yet. "Once you have finished the conversation and heard your final guidance, you will know to put on the red jacket."

I awoke feeling warm and safe and approved, even if I didn't have a new house or a finished book.

The idea that I was being invisibly guided, that there was a red, gold-tasseled jacket for me to wear when I was ready, stayed with me. Even though I don't believe in spirit guides, it did seem clear that when I stayed aware in the present what I needed came to me. I knew that I was exceptionally lucky for the freedom Jim had given me and that the job, the one that had been so wrong for me, was really a gift.

I had taken it a couple of months before learning about Jim's cancer diagnosis, leaving a heavy-duty senior management position. Starting with his lung surgery and increasingly as he grew sicker, my new employers let me work from home and reduced my work-load – this would not have been possible in my previous job. How would I have handled Jim's needs while visiting clients in Florida, Colorado, or Ohio? How could I have directed a team of ten when all of my energy had been channeled into keeping track of doctors?

Even more important, the job that I'd gotten kicked out of ended up connecting me to the people who made my escape from 9 to 5 possible: The boss who made me release my death grip on a job that didn't suit me and then offered a small but steady supply of freelance work. The interactive agency that wanted me as a strategy and content consultant. The co-worker who moved on to a university where she wanted me for branded copywriting and thought I should meet her sister, Carole, who topped my list of new friends.

"I can't tell you what a good thing it is that I got fired," I gushed to her over a cranberry-orange scone and cup of fresh roasted coffee on a balmy May afternoon. The last of the daffodil blooms were nodding at the Scholar's Inn Bakehouse on the Courthouse Square, and the redbud trees were showing off the purple tinge of their rosy pink flowers.

Carole adjusted the knobby purple scarf at the neck of her jacket and leaned forward as if she wanted to hear more.

"I really think I can pull off my little business," I said. "My third and best try at entrepreneurship. All the pieces are falling into place. What's great about it is that I don't have to market. I know all these people, they know my work, and most of it I can do online. Hardly ever have to drive to the city."

I looked across the tables full of people who were reading books and munching on sandwiches, waving to friends walking by, and zoning out on their laptops. This world had been here all along, but without me. I had been so wrapped up in my career, traveling, living in the country, dealing with a dying man, that I had never had the time to appreciate the town I lived in.

"My sister always told me that you knew too much about marketing, that those people didn't know how to use you," said Carole.

"It's kind of her to say that," I replied, trying to shake off the unease that always arose when I thought about that job, even though I knew that getting it and leaving it had been the right things to do. "I'm lucky to have met your sister there. Lucky that she liked me despite my demise. Lucky she moved on to her big-time job and that she gives me projects." I tossed a few crumbs down for the sparrows hopping between the tables and then looked up to catch Carole's eye. "And lucky she introduced you to me."

"Luck? Or making lemonade from lemons?" Carole asked generously. "I think you have a feeling for how to wiggle into the overlooked spaces."

"I don't know." I fell silent, trying to sense if she would think the feelings that were stirring inside me were silly. I went on to cautiously explain a thought I'd been pondering. "It has all worked out better than I could have ever expected. It was the worst job ever, such a personally degrading fall from career grace, but everything about it feels cosmic. Coming when I needed it while Jim was sick. And forcing me later to completely let go so that I could do well in this little business."

"One thing leads to another," said Carole. "You sound so together."

"'Together' is pushing it," I said with a laugh and scooted my chair back to give myself some space. "But better than numb and flatlined like I was last year. I can get from point A to point B and maybe stumble on toward Point Z."

"I can't imagine you ever flatlined. Flatlined for you is like percolating for someone else. I'm getting a refill. Want more coffee?" Carole held her mug aloft and extended her other hand in my direction.

"Sure, thanks – decaf." I handed her my white ceramic mug and watched her trim figure slip into the café.

I no longer had the eye twitch, but I wasn't taking any chances. I couldn't shake this strange sensation that something big was afoot in my life. I felt extra alive and found myself gushing in exclamation points. And I had a feeling that I simply was not in charge anymore. My fingers had been pried not only from my job but from the grasp I'd always had on life. It was as if I was following my life instead of leading it. Walking calmly toward the red jacket that was waiting for me. Sometimes I could almost hear the wheel of my fortune creaking, my universe deliberately rearranging itself, and I knew that Carole was part of it.

She was new in town and experimenting with people, trying out different configurations of personalities. I hoped she would hang on to me and continue to drag me along with her as she unearthed a Bloomington that was unlike the one I knew. Last December, Carole had convinced me to take a writing class. It was over a different cup of coffee in the same café.

"You should enroll," she'd told me. "It's a little woo-woo, but you might like it. The women are interesting. The weekly deadlines make me write. I end up thinking about things I might not on my own."

"I do need a new head," I'd said, recalling the files I had found over the winter. Two fat manila folders with my name written on the tabs in Jim's loose, pressed-hard, penciled handwriting, a strong curlicue flourish on the C. In no particular order, my old letters, postcards, notes, and drawings from years ago.

The witty, smart woman in these old files was so far from the current floundering me. She was so well read, up to speed on the latest science news, able to make effortless references to the contemporary issues of the day, and comfortable with her opinions – purposefully oblique, articulate, radical, and sexy.

I had read several of Jim's books over the winter but quit because the head was an old head. Graham Greene, Gore Vidal, John

McPhee – all good, but old. I wanted a new, contemporary head. Scanning over the list of the *New York Times* notable books, the authors were unknown to me. Same thing when flipping through the *Atlantic Monthly* or the *New Yorker.* I needed to get looped in to the modern head. I needed to fill in that still vacant, collapsed section of me that had grown in response to Jim. But who was the me without him?

Carole had never met Jim or the Jim me. When she saw me, the un-Jim me, she saw a me that hadn't existed before. I liked her push-back. She was a new hand to clap against, albeit a gentler hand than Jim's.

"It's a good group," Carole had said. "It can't hurt to try out a class."

I doled out a few hundred dollars from my carefully guarded savings account and started a Wednesday night class in January, a month before my job swoop, driving like a maniac through ice and rain to get back to Bloomington on time from Indianapolis. I would zip into the parking lot behind the big white house where the class was held and rush up the rickety steps in the dark to sign in and collect the handouts for the evening, often slipping in last to join a dozen or so women sitting in a circle in the upstairs front room. I'd smile nervously, put a cup of hot ginger-lemon tea on the floor next to my purse, and struggle to balance notebook and papers in my lap so that I could be ready for the woo-woo candle coming quickly toward me.

I was supposed to have a word ready to say when the candle got to me. "Checking in" it was called. A moment to focus and settle before the class began.

I never knew what might come out of my mouth. Often it was something like "recalibrating," or "discombobulated." It didn't matter, because whatever I said, a calm space would open before me. This surprised cynical me, but not nearly as much as I enjoyed feeling the warm, soft fingertips of the next woman as I transferred the candle from my hands to hers. Safe human contact.

After the candle passing there was the reading of a poem, like these lines from a poem by the award-winning poet Mary Oliver:

"Just a minute," said a voice in the weeds.
So I stood still
in the day's exquisite early morning light
and so I didn't crush with my great feet
any small or unusual thing just happening to pass by

It had been decades since I'd had poetry in my life. The women in the class wrote serrated stories of family upheaval, sweet love, and bitter tragedy that made Jim's death seem less awful. They wrote poems about life gathering itself, regrouping, and reseeding.

The group would have welcomed my stories of Jim – of our years together, his illness, his death, my insane buzz, my career implosion, but I didn't want to talk about any of it. I was sick of it. I wanted different thoughts in my head and found myself writing long, convoluted paragraphs heavy with description, trying my hand at a mystery novel that I was preparing to take to the writer's conference at Indiana University in the summer.

While other women worked on what they were feeling, I worked on how my words fit together in an imaginary world. I didn't want to feel anymore. I was all felt out. Instead I wanted to know how did *heads bobbing like shore birds* go with *sultry, white-toothed smiles*? I wanted to think about colors (*fuchsia toenails*), gestures (*he moved his hand away*), and smells (*a sharp whiff of wet salt and seaweed*). It was like rediscovering the world, only not the real world, but one that lived in my keyboard. A facsimile. One where I could delete and start again.

Every session ended with the ding of a meditation gong. That was fine, but the singing circle that came next dipped so far into the woo-woo that I could barely do it. Standing in a circle (of course), holding hands, we sang several swaying rounds of a chant in smiling, tentative harmonies: *There's a river of birds in migration, a nation of women with wings.*

There were some nights that I found comfort in the woman-song chanting, but mostly I felt conflicted. Sometimes I wolfed down the classes and the hand-holding, hungry for contact. New ideas multiplied in my head like zucchini on the vine in July. Other times the cloying woo-woo was alienating.

Despite the invisible guidance I felt, the perimeter of ashes I had cast down, and the roaring hole to hell that had been in Jim's room, I was not interested in group-think spirituality. I'd had plenty of communal thinking back in my hippie days, and I didn't need any more. I didn't even want to be a team player, much less a member of a consciousness-raising community. I wanted to find my own way, define my own life.

And poor Mona, my fictional heroine who was being railroaded wrongly for embezzlement, and her shadow counterpart, Bella the tattoo artist, were both out of place among all the insightful odes to mothers, the gullies of sorrows, the measurement of time, the terrors of breast cancer, and the backwash of rape.

I was an outsider. It's a role I knew well, but one that doesn't get any more comfortable while lingering on the outside of in-crowd exchanges about what happened last Sunday at the Unitarian Church, or just beyond the fringe of familiar tête-à-têtes about children, or set aside from the conversation that started at dinner before class.

The core of the group was tight. So when one writer packed up, teary-eyed, to move out of town with her husband for his new faculty position, a hole was rent. Everyone, even those of us who were peripheral, was invited to attend her going-away party. We were asked to bring something to read aloud and then give to the departing woman.

The afternoon party was in a big home with high cathedral ceilings, walls of angular windows overlooking a wooded ravine, and substantial furniture. In my new hibiscus-red batik dress and big earrings, I nervously balanced a plate of salad, brie, hummus, and pita bread in one hand and held a glass of wine in the other, sure I would spill. I arranged a smile on my face and waited, listening to the murmur of familiarity and fondness while shifting self-consciously in my chair.

Clockwise, in a circle, the women began to read to their departing friend. Poems and paragraphs on friendship and change; some they'd written, some from books. I realized the poem I had brought was off topic and lightweight. It was about writing, not the change that was happening. I'd been so immersed in myself that I hadn't even gotten the point of the gathering. Then my social fussing became irrelevant when the woman across from me began to read.

It was an essay likening the changes in life to a series of trapeze swings. About how we focus on quickly getting to the next thing, missing the growth in the transition, in the space between letting go of one bar and grabbing the next.

> The void in between? That's just a scary, confusing, disorienting "nowhere" that must be gotten through as fast and as unconsciously as possible. What a waste! . . . The transition zones in our lives are incredibly rich places. They should be honored, even savored. Yes, with all the pain and fear and feelings of being out of control that can . . . accompany transitions, they are still the most alive, most growth-filled, passionate, expansive moments in our lives.
>
> And so, transformation of fear may have nothing to do with making fear go away, but rather with giving ourselves permission to "hang out" in the transition between the trapeze bars. Transforming our need to grab that new bar, any bar, is allowing ourselves to dwell in the only place where change really happens. It can be terrifying. It can also be enlightening, in the true sense of the word. Hurtling through the void, we just may learn how to fly.

If I believed in such things, I would have thought this could be my dream's final guidance. But I didn't need a dream to recognize the click of truth when I heard it. Like the trumpet of a Heavenly Blue Morning Glory bud opens to the warm sun, a knowing inside of me unlocked. I was in the In Between void of transition. I had been rushing around to get to the next thing, the next me, when it wasn't needed. I could linger in the In Between for as long as it took. It was suddenly clear. My job was to stay in the present and to pay attention. And my present was this room full of women who were willing to put up with me, who were teaching me without knowing it, and who didn't care if the poem I brought was about writing instead of change. All they wanted me to do was participate.

12

The Point of Surrender

It was a July summer day spent timelessly in the garden, wandering from bed to bed with a general, but not strict, vegetative agenda. Following narrow leaves and stems down to root clusters, I untangled and pulled thin, weedy grass from the clump of bronze ajuga and lemon thyme that was planted around the blue and yellow flag bog iris. The light citrus smell of thyme drifted upward.

This kind of delicate weeding always links me back to the eons of women with their infinite tasks of details – weaving, berry picking, stitching, sorting grain. There's a concentration to it that hushes the constant patter of the brain and moves one into a timeless zone. Scooting along inch by inch on my butt, I separated leaves, carefully uprooting only the grass. How expertly the grass wove itself into the roots and stems of the ajuga and tiny-leafed thyme – as if it knew it had a better chance for survival if it was complicated, perhaps thinking I might never get around to such a meticulous task. Unlucky for the grass, this bed was one of a few places I kept weeded. Mostly things were jumbling into one another in the gardens.

And things were complicated and jumbled in my brain as well. Although I was trying to stay in the present, I wanted a new present. A new now. A different house, one in town. A different pattern to my days. A civilized and obedient garden. A different me. Not a recluse on the hick side of the county, but part of the artsy intellectual town crowd who went to plays and sipped wine while listening to jazz. A different life altogether. But that would be moving on, and I was not moving on, or at least not very quickly. I was dwelling in the In Between, whether I wanted to or not.

The house had been for sale since my job swoop, and housing values were falling like whirligigs from maples, twirling down, down, down. If only I had not listened to the advice for widows (you must wait a year before making any big decisions) and sold right after Jim died. If only I had not sunk all that money into remodeling. Even a rock-bottom, handy-man-special price last year would have been more than what I could get this year after fixing it up. That is, if I could sell it at all. The showings had dried up. People were scared to buy houses, afraid of the market free fall. My offer on a cute house in town, contingent on selling this house, had been turned down. I had to face the possibility that it might take more than a year to sell. That I was going to have to stay out here, working alone, living alone, and often unwilling to make the twenty-mile round trip into town. If I was going to stay, how this place operated had to change. I couldn't keep up. I couldn't do my chores and Jim's chores too.

I stopped weeding, brushed the dirt from my hands, and nudged a napping Lila, who was stretched out in the warm sun beside me. "Don't you wish you had opposable thumbs?" She banged her tail and lazily lifted her head. Jealous Diggity hurried over from her spot under the pines and eagerly interjected her wet nose, smearing my glasses as if to say, "Ask me, ask me! We do, we do! We wish we had opposable thumbs. But if we had them, we'd do better things with them than sit here for hours pulling grass." Digs danced around me, hoping I would throw a stick; Lila jumped up. The two of them pushed me over in dog enthusiasm.

Stretching my aching back, I got up and wandered into the house, where a pile of real estate files were stacked on the dining room table. The sturdy oak table had been an antique shop find, sold at a tremendous discount due to its terrible condition. I ran my hand along its swirly tiger-grain top. Jim had rebuilt it and sanded smooth its roughened surface and then turned it over to me for fine sanding, conditioning, staining, and finishing. Those days were gone. Any table I got from here on out would have to be in better shape.

I pulled out one of the spindle-back oak chairs and sat down heavily with a glass of cold water. In the file in front of me were the real estate detail sheets of the houses I'd considered and the multi-page offer that had been turned down the day before. "There's no point in making any more offers in this climate until you have an offer on your house," my realtor had said. On top of the papers in the folder was my New House Essentials list. It was actually the same list I had made seven years ago, before Jim talked me into buying this needy house.

I'd gotten my open floor plan and light, lots of storage and plenty of garage space. The dogs got Dog Paradise. I had a nice kitchen. And it was outrageously private and quiet. But I had completely bombed out when it came to low maintenance, no fixer-upper, and little mowing – all things that had fallen into Jim's category.

*   *   *

That first spring after we bought the house – two and a half years before Jim finally moved in – it took only a dribble of rain and a few days of warm weather before the grass took off with an intensity unseen in city lawns.

"I'll mow it, no problem," Jim had said as he rolled my lawn mower out of the pole barn on a Saturday. He mowed the lawn at his house in town. He mowed the lawns of his elderly neighbor widows in exchange for pies and pot roasts. So mowing our two acres on a Saturday seemed like nothing to him. He was already mowing at least that much in town, no big deal.

"You won't make a dent with that," I'd said, waving off his confidence while he filled the tank with gasoline. "That's pasture fescue out there, not bluegrass or rye; it's tough and the ground is uneven. It'll take you forever."

"I'll see you at happy hour." Jim laughed.

"I'll be working out by the road," I said, turning to the ten flats of wintercreeper, rolls of landscape fabric, and a small mountain of mulch that were waiting by the wheelbarrow. "Once I get the grass killed and the ground cover going, you won't have to mow there. It's too dangerous; there's no shoulder. Sooner or later you'll be crushed by cars flying down that hilly curve."

"What are we having for happy hour?" Jim looked away to run a wire brush over the end of the mower's spark plug.

"Sidecars," I said. "It's cognac, Grand Marnier, and lemon juice. Named after the motorcycle sidecar, from the 1920s." Happy hour in the Sunset Lounge, the garden shed's paddock-patio, was a new twist on our Saturday nights now that going to dinner in town was a freaking expedition. We were working our way through classic cocktails, a weekly toasting of gin fizzes or whiskey sours as the orange summer sun descended behind the trees.

"Catch you in the Sunset Lounge." Jim grinned, securing the spark plug, and pulling the cord. The mower sputtered to life.

Picking my way through Miller Lite beer cans, Big Gulp cups, and White Castle bags, I spread out the alleged weed-blocking fabric over the already knee-deep, mounding grass on the slope by the road. I began to wonder about the wisdom of the venture as the plastic holding pegs broke whenever they hit rocks, which were everywhere. Maybe I should have killed the grass first so that the fabric would lie flat, or at least mowed it. Too late. I punched holes in the lumpy blanket of black that stretched about a hundred feet and planted more than three hundred wintercreeper starts. It's an Asian native, a woody evergreen vine also known as euonymus that's considered a bully invasive and shunned by the more ecologically correct. But bully invasive was fine with me; I wanted something that could out-invade anything that might need mowing. Alas, it would prove to be no match to the absolutely evil pasture fescue, johnsongrass, and crab grass that took root in the top of the landscape fabric. I should have simply planted – for a fraction of the price and effort – common orange daylilies, also known as ditch lilies for their ability to squeeze out any weed in a roadside ditch. But on that spring day, I was sure I was a clever gardener.

Late afternoon, hot, with prickly red arms and a sore back, I walked toward the puttering sound of the lawnmower until I found Jim mowing in the back pasture. Vast stretches of grass were still untouched. As I approached him, he released the handle of the mower, and it shut off.

"Ready for your sidecar?" I asked, pulling off my new cotton gloves, their cheery little blue flowers lost under a layer of black grime. "I'm done for the day. I'll mulch tomorrow."

"This isn't really a lawn," Jim said as he mopped his face with his T-shirt. "It's a fucking cow pasture. There are molehills everywhere. I wish I had a tractor."

The next weekend Jim and I plopped our credit cards down next to each other on the counter at Sears and soon were unloading a *Consumer Reports*–recommended green lawn tractor with Jim's name written in black marker on masking tape stuck to the back of the seat.

The tape with his name is still there.

We held this configuration for four summers. I gardened. Jim mowed.

I put in a vegetable garden big enough to feed a farm family of four. Jim mowed.

By the split rail fences on each side of the driveway I planted pink, white, and scarlet peonies and purple, mauve, and magenta clematis vines. Jim mowed.

In the west end of Dog Paradise, I planted ornamental grasses in an attempt to disguise a security light pole that was as big as a tree and its support wires, which were covered in bright yellow plastic. Soon I had also scatter-planted a dogwood tree, a dwarf sour cherry tree, a snowball bush, and a curly willow. Jim mowed. And complained.

"You're making it hard to mow. It used to be straight lines; now's there's all this crap in the way," he'd chided.

"In the fullness," I had patiently explained. "The shrubs will grow big and take up space. You'll have less to mow."

"Better be soon, because it's a pain in the butt," Jim grumped, and mowed.

Then during the summer between chemo and surgery, Jim's mowing got bizarre.

I would be fighting weeds out by the road or picking bushels of green beans when I would hear him bark, *Fucker!* I'd stop and tilt my head to listen, wondering if I'd heard right. I'd go back to hunting for beans hiding in the stems under the leaves and *"Cocksucker!"* would echo across the way. The first time this happened, I had asked him about it at happy hour in the Sunset Lounge.

"Why all the swearing?"

"What swearing?" he'd asked.

"While you were mowing."

"I don't know what you're talking about," Jim had said, giving me a strange look.

And then he began to mow in the wrong direction, circling inward instead of outward, blowing grass into deep mounds of clippings that would burn big brown spots in the lawn. I would run over, waving my arms and shouting, "Go the other way!"

He would smile and change directions, but later he'd be back going the wrong way, cursing as he went. I would always end up raking the clippings and wheel-barrowing them to the vegetable garden.

It was hours of work, and I already had the garden mulched with newspaper and straw – a simple one-time operation. But the cuttings had to be moved.

"Why have you stopped blowing the clippings out instead of in?" I would ask him.

"You just don't understand," he'd say, rubbing his chin. "It's the only direction I can mow."

"Like the day at the Tibetan Cultural Center when the monk told you to walk in the other direction because you were unwinding your karma?"

"No nothing like that."

Wound or unwound karma, he never could believe that he was swearing, and he could only go one way. Either way, with Jim dead, I was stuck with the mowing.

*   *   *

I don't know why people love to mow, but they do. Especially on riding mowers. Maybe they find a certain peace out there in the wind and sun, slowly driving in circles in the undulating green. Maybe they enjoy the slow tour of their properties, taking measure of their land and gardens. Maybe it makes them feel like cowboys. Or maybe they like riding around on a little tractor. Maybe it's the only time they get to be alone.

Amazingly, there is a whole subculture of mowing. There's a TV cartoon show featuring a beer-guzzling wiseacre on his riding mower. A *Lawn Mower Racing Mania* video game. The Lawn Mower Brigade has marched in the Indiana University homecoming parade, and the Almost Precision Lawnmower Drill Team has performed in neighboring Brown County's Spring Blossom Parade. There is actually a U.S. Lawnmower Racing Association.

But it's not for me. I hate mowing. It's four hours wasted not gardening, or not walking in the woods, or not driving into town to do some undefined but cool thing.

Faced with potentially years of mowing the unsalable property, my brain listed toward escape schemes. What if I just didn't mow? Or just mowed Dog Paradise and the front lawn? Let the outer lawns return to woods? Oh, no. That would be too simple.

I closed the real estate file and unrolled the two-by-three-foot garden plan I had started in the spring. Just because I was living in the In Between didn't mean I was planless. I am a planner by instinct and over the decades have made hundreds, if not thousands of them. Marketing plans, publicity plans, revenue plans, business plans, career plans, vacation plans, house-buying plans, and garden plans. Some of them wonderfully effective, others no more than logical pathways to failure.

Once when starting a soon-to-fail Internet portal and marketing business, I proudly showed the business plan and sales forecast spread sheets to my accountant, asking her for an opinion. "I think you know how to use Excel software really well," she said tactfully.

I know that plans are not reality, that they are only a sketch of a possible future. I know that when the future morphs into the present, it comes with its own agenda. But a good plan, especially one that thoroughly explores the pros and cons of choices, helps you think so that you don't have to knee-jerk your way through everything. But I am also capable of wide-eyed planning my way into disaster, selectively ignoring the obvious. This is not a flaw that's exclusive to me – everyone does it. But even knowing that, I can't always tell a good plan from a bad one until it hits reality.

I weighed down the curling paper corners of the garden plan with books and files. So far it wasn't a really a plan. It was a map of my world as it was, not as I wished it would be, on sturdy translucent vellum, blown up and traced in pencil from an aerial photo.

In the center of the two-acre rectangle were the hard-scapes – house, garage, barn, fences. The garden shed was set back, up on the hill behind the house. Little circles represented the wind-breaking stands of pine and spruce that shielded the house from pry-ing eyes and divided Dog Paradise from the back pasture. The red azalea at the corner of the garage. Larger circles noted the cooling yellow poplar to the east of the house and silver maple to the west. The old apple tree. That was pretty much all that was here when I started five years ago.

Since then I've added the clumps of ornamental grasses along fence lines, by the road, around the security light. The struggling wintercreeper on the slope. The curly willow that had gone from twig to twenty feet. The clematis on the rail fences next to the peonies. The curving French drain that led to the pineapple mint, horsetails, and hydrangeas of a rain garden. The long stretch of thyme, where hundreds of double daffodils bloomed in the spring. The stone step garden that bisected the back hill. The veggie patch. The raspberry bushes, the pawpaw trees, the cherry tree, and the little dogwood.

And still it was mostly grass.

But it wouldn't be for long. I had a plan.

*   *   *

The next week a low-key, stocky young man walked with me over the vast lawn while cardinals bobbed red and *birdie-birdied* in the fir trees at the edge of the pasture and the love song of the cicadas throbbed. An offhanded comment by a prairie-less friend had stirred me to call him. His company specialized in something magical called *native plant communities*.

My mind raced as he described wiping out most of the grass. "We'll kill the existing pasture grasses with herbicide and then come in a week or so later with drill-seeding equipment to plant native species." He handed me a plant list that made my list-maker heart swell. Little bluestem, Virginia wild rye, bottlebrush, and beak grasses, plus butterfly weed, columbine, purple coneflower, nodding wild onion, tall bellflower, dense blazing star, black-eyed Susans, wild bergamot, downy wood mint, foxglove beard tongue, hoary vervain, compass plant, and a score of other prairie flowers. It was as if he had sprinkled fairy dust on me.

Starry-eyed, where the accursed lawn now grew I imagined finches and swallowtails flittering across an expanse of yellow and pink flowers bowing their heads in the breeze. In the Sunset Lounge, a relaxed me was chilling with a novel, an icy gin and tonic on the table while the mower grew cobwebs in the pole barn.

I pushed aside his comment about killing the grass with herbicide to zero in on the other lovely words he used, like *biodiversity* and *ecological restoration*. Trying not to pile insult on injury, Jim and I had banned herbicides, still made with the same ingredients as Agent Orange.

The ecologist and I walked and pointed, talking about the land, the seep, the swale in the back pasture. I managed not to mention that Jim had been the mower and that he was dead. "Let's wrap the Prairie around the sides and back of the property, starting at the road," I said. This would take out over an acre of grass and slice two hours off my mowing time.

"We can customize the seed mix to your wet areas and improve the condition of the pasture swale so that the water flows away from the house even better," he said.

I was impressed with his knowledge.

"It will take about three years for it to start looking like a prairie," he said as I stood in the wiry fescue. The breathtaking floral display of my future overrode the executive functions of my frontal cortex, where the ability to recognize future consequences resulting from current actions resides.

"The first year, you won't even notice most of the plants; they'll be busy putting down taproots," he continued while running his hand over his close-clipped beard. "To help it, you'll have to kill tree saplings – poplar, locust, oak, sycamore, sassafras, maple, and sumac – as well as multiflora roses, wild blackberry canes, Canadian thistle, catbriers, and fescue as they try to get a foothold."

I laughed lightly, thinking that would be nothing compared to mowing, and said, "Well, that's no problem." He delivered a quick glance of incredulousness, which I dismissed. Instead of being enchanted by the fantasy of the Prairie, I should have been alert to that glance and asked more about it. I should have noticed that I was selectively ignoring critical information instead of la-la-la-ing ahead. Then he would have told me that my mowing time would be replaced with hours of eliminating the scores of non-native, pioneering plants that wanted to call a newly disturbed plot of land home. That I would spend Saturdays attending classes on prairie maintenance. That I would mix gallons of Agent Orange–ish herbicide with red food dye so that I could mark which cut saplings had been treated and which had not, because an untreated cut sapling branches out twice its size. That my hands would bathtub-wrinkle inside steamy latex gloves as I tried to avoid contact with the poisons. That I would ultimately name the prairies Tick Acres for the gazillions of dog, deer, and lone star ticks that latched on to suck my blood and threaten me with Lyme disease and Rocky Mountain spotted fever while I slaved.

Then I would have backed away from the idea of a prairie, for I would have realized that I was trading mowing for the artificial maintenance of a prairie where a woods wanted to grow. I would have remembered that southern Indiana isn't flat prairie land; it's hilly woods.

But I didn't. He walked away with a check from my savings account in his pocket and dates for the killing and seed drilling in his electronic calendar.

It wasn't an impulsive decision. It was a careful, considered investment. I'd read up on prairies, visited other plots that had been converted to prairie, and thought hard about spending the money. My trouble was that I'm a fool for the romantic notions of gardens and in love with the idea of transforming the common into the extraordinary. It's why I'm a sucker for garden catalogs.

After he left I rolled out my garden plan over the dining room table and drew in the *U* shape around the perimeter of the property and marked it *Prairie*. A zone of nondescript blah was now a labeled destination, along with the Sunset Lounge and Dog Paradise. I penciled in *Veggie Heaven* over the long rectangle where a truckload of plowed-in-compost-rich soil, along with my hours of tilling and mulching, had converted pasture to productive garden.

Cirrus jumped up onto the table and stretched out over the new Prairie.

My pencil wavered over the west end of Dog Paradise, where the security light reigned. My efforts to eliminate the lawn and disguise the forty-foot light pole with its brilliant yellow support lines had been only marginally successful. It could have been named *Plot of Circular Thinking*. My plantings had not made the mowing easier as I had promised Jim. It took forever to mow around the isolated trees and shrubs. Grass grew long and shaggy by the trunks I never had time to trim.

I sketched in aspirational oblong ovals of connected beds around the shrubs and trees and a grass path exactly the width of the mower. Red and yellow twig dogwood and old-fashioned snowball hydrangeas, more yellow forsythia, twining bittersweet, and large swaths of black-eyed Susans to fill in the haphazard, weedy clumps of pink French pussy willows on the fence borders.

By the next month, after the heavy seed drill tractors had come and gone across the front lawn to the Prairie, there was yet another mountain of mulch in the driveway and a huddled mass of shrubs and plants in two- and three-gallon black plastic pots. The surrounding land outside the Dog Paradise fence was herbicide brown, awaiting germination. Inside the fence, the dogs stood in the thick green grass wondering what could possibly be next.

* * *

It was the third week of digging mud-sucking shovelfuls of heavy, clay-laden dirt, of muscling bushes bigger than me into the wheelbarrow and then into the holes, of enduring the wheelbarrow's persistent flat tire and the long mulch treks from the end of the drive, when I wondered if I had made a mistake with this section of new garden.

A thin sun was dipping below the horizon, and the dusk had thickened with tiny mosquitoes that bit my ears without mercy. My tired fingers were shriveled and numb in soggy work gloves. I jammed the shovel into the clay with my work boot but couldn't lift it out. The leaden, putty-colored soil held to itself and the deep roots of the tall fescue resisted. My boot, caked with heavy mud, must have weighed an extra five pounds. Heaving a sigh, I sank to the wet ground.

I slapped first one ear and then the other at the hounding mosquitoes. The buzz of urgency hovered over me, my old companion come calling. I swatted and dodged, unimpressed with its lure of madness. Only a tiny percent of the nursery plants were in the ground. The mud and mess made it even harder to mow. The season was advancing, and I was not. There were not enough hours in my weeks to wrestle this mud and run my business.

In my past, desperation borne at the discovery of miscalculation would gather in invisible piles of uncertainty at my feet like dandelion puff seeds in the corners.

But no longer. In the In Between I dealt with what came. I couldn't guess at what I might be refusing to see. I couldn't anticipate when a complication might derail me, when a body might betray me. I couldn't know the future. All I could do was surrender to the moment.

I gave up on prying out the shovel's load, slid it out of the impossible muck, and took it back to the pole barn for the simple clarity of washing clay off the smooth metal blade.

The next day I called a landscaping company.

A tanned, lanky Nordic man, his first year out of college, came out to walk the yard with me. As with the ecologist, I pointed; I told the stories of the soil and plants. I explained the slowly germinating Prairie and the idea behind shrubs versus lawn. I wrote him a check from my savings account, another investment.

The next week he brought me a not-to-scale plan with my name misspelled across the top that ignored existing plantings and trees. It was as if he was trying to plant from a template of a future that had no resemblance to the present. I gave the plan back and tried to explain again what I wanted. Looping grass paths exactly the width of the mower. Existing beds expanded and connected to new ones.

Finally he looked at me with a broad smile of understanding and said, "Oh, you want a park."

Yes! That's what I wanted. A park where I could stroll and linger on benches. After he left I unrolled the garden plan and penciled in *Park* on the west end of Dog Paradise. But that seemed too plain. Parks aren't called parks. They are named for important points in history. I erased *Park* and carefully wrote *Point of Surrender*.

By mid-July the Point of Surrender landscapers came and went. Unlike the slowly evolving Prairie that would ultimately be my folly, their work changed everything immediately. Six tons of river gravel, four tons of tumbled creek gravel, twelve yards of mulch, eleven ornamental grasses, thirty-six bushes, and more, all put in on one day. All moved across the front lawn in big trucks.

In the violet, mosquito-ridden twilight after the workers left, the dogs and I walked on the grass walkway that encircled a river-stone-mulched oval island of bushes that had joined the curly willow and ornamental grasses by the security light. The yellow support lines were now invisible. Noses to the ground, the girls inhaled the new beds while I slowly strolled the looping path by the clumps of "Limelight" hydrangea, purple ninebark, Miscanthus grass, forsythia, red and yellow twig dogwood, and burning bushes. Accent curves of tidy, green boxwood shrubs guided my way. Periwinkle momentarily held sway where fescue had once defeated me. There were two half-moons of decorative gravel waiting for garden benches.

For a moment, everything was in order.

13

The Shitty Truth

The sun crept through the blinds as Lila's eager black nose nuzzled me awake. I snuggled against the comfort of my grandmother's flower garden quilt, glancing at the clock. The rich, dark greenness of the white pines tossing in the wind against a clear blue sky filled the bedroom windows. Then a Diggity dog nose. Cirrus romped across me. I was up.

It would be a busy day. I had a deadline for a website project, but more important, I needed to get to the Monroe County Health Department in town to pick up my copies of the septic field plan before they closed at four o'clock. And I was meeting Carole mid-afternoon on the square for coffee.

The septic system had always been a little mysterious to me. It's one of those things about country living. You have one, just like you are forced to either have an electric stove or an ugly propane gas tank in your yard.

The previous owner had proudly toured one side of our giant front lawn with us, talking about how big the septic field is now, pointing this way and that as he and Jim matched manly strides. "Since we replaced it, you'll never have the problems we did," he'd said. Following behind, I made little cryptic notes. Listening to their discussion, I jotted down numbers and notes to accompany a loose drawing on a tiny scrap of paper. I'd given this paper to Jim. He was the guy, and septic systems are a guy thing. In our new shared-house ownership, he was the one who called for the honey truck; I was the one who planted a patch of blue lyme grass around the access hatches to the tanks and considered my work done. Septics weren't a guy thing for me anymore.

Most people don't even think about their septic system unless black muck starts oozing up in the yard or sewer water bubbles up in the bathtub – giving new meaning to the music of Robert Bradley and the Blackwater Surprise. Some, inviting the blackwater blues into their lives, never have their tanks pumped out.

Not us. The Royal Flush tank-pumping honey truck, emblazoned with their slogan, *It Beats a Full House,* had been here twice in five years. But I wasn't sure where the pipes were in the field. I knew you are not supposed to drive anything larger than a riding lawn mower over the field. And what about the inlet pipes? Where were they? With blind faith I had directed a sixteen-ton bucket truck over that side of the front lawn so that a crew could take down a three-foot-wide, hollow sycamore tree that was about to crash through the power lines onto the house. I had pointed the way for dump trucks full of Point of Surrender creek gravel and for the heavy tractors used to seed drill the Prairie. Each time, I uncertainly instructed them where to drive, hoping pipes were not being crushed beneath wheels. And then there was this lush patch of grass just beyond the tanks. Was that from current standing wastewater in the field, from recently crushed pipes, or from the implied failure of the earlier septic system?

My inquiries started indoors. I went down into the laundry room and puzzled in front of the septic pump controls, trying to remember what I was supposed to do if the pump stopped and the alarm went off. Friends had warned me against using the garbage disposal, saying that food matter would clog the drain field. I found out that you can use the garbage disposal if you treat it as if it were another person living in the house, that good drain hygiene – no oils or fats – is essential. I wondered if I also should let yellow mellow and flush down brown.

I started reading websites, learning terms like *scum layer* and *liquid effluent*. I learned that waste is pumped to a two-chambered tank where the unthinkable solids settle and the disgusting scum floats. Things are anaerobically digested, and some awful liquid flows to the second chamber and then seeps out in a less stinky form through long trenches of rock and perforated pipe that stretched somewhere out in the front lawn, maybe where the trucks drove over.

In Jim's files I'd found the little scrap of paper from the owner's tour with the sketch of my very own small-scale sewage treatment plant. In my scratchy writing were the numbers about how big the field was and how deep the fingers of the five trenches were. There was an *X* that noted the location of the blue spruce in front of the house. Pretty cryptic. In a flash of brilliance, I called the county health department and ordered a copy of the system plan from when it had been replaced. Today I was picking up the plan, after the dump and burgers.

I swung my feet off the bed to the floor. Both dog noses begging to be let out. "Okay, okay. I have to pee too," I told the girls as they hurried me to the back door. "Today, sweet pound cakes, we'll go for a ride in the truck." They stopped and twirled around in unison at the words "go for a ride." "Later," I said as I opened the door for them. Some humans think that dogs can't understand the concept of *later*, that they only understand the now, but my dogs do. Waiting for me to fulfill the promise, to head for the truck, added flavor to their day. I never lie to them about later.

Jim's pickup truck was mine now. Not just by title but by action as well. I had made the new cheery yellow and green sunflower cotton seat cover that fit tightly over the uncomfortable rip in the bench seat. Under the hood there was a new temperature-sending unit, thanks to my roadside breakdown and emergency towing incident. The rusted-out bottom corners of the cab were newly filled with expandable yellow spray foam and painted over, thanks to a tactic I had learned online. The peeling paint on the hood and roof were sanded and touched up with the faded silver pickup truck spray paint that I had stumbled across on a random visit to the Walmart over in Spencer.

Still, Jim's friends did a double-take when they saw me driving my de-Jimmed truck. No one seemed to remember that I used to drive it around when Jim was alive too. He had been dead for a year and a half; they should be used to seeing me in the truck by now. Besides, it was my truck. Jim would never have a truck with a sunflower seat cover.

The truck was my vehicle of choice for the dirty occasions of my life: trips to the greenhouse, monthly trash and recycling trips, hiking, kayaking, and everything muddy. And anything muddy or dirty was high adventure, according to the dogs, who never forgot that the truck also went on random vacations when Jim had been around. They kept an eye on the truck, hoping every day for an outing.

The poor girls suffered because of my boring ways. They watched me type for hours on the computer or scoot around on my butt, weeding. They thought I didn't understand what was important in life, because if I did we'd be in the truck heading for a good time.

That afternoon, after pushing the send button on my project, I walked out to the pole barn and looked toward the overhang where the truck was parked. That's all it took. The girls ran to the gate and sat in quivering attention, being good dogs in hopes of adventure. Holding still, small yips escaping, they sat while I opened the gate, looking into my eyes for a sign of their release. At my "Okay, let's go" they burst through the gate to the back of the truck, skidding to a stop, and then bouncing in excitement as they waited for me to catch up. Their excitement flickered over me and through my fingers as I lifted up the horizontal door to the camper shell (with the broken supports yet to be fixed) and rested it on my head while jimmying the stuck (yet to be fixed) latch of the rear gate. They impatiently whined as I found the wooden board in the bed of the truck and jammed it in to hold the upper door. That door was a fooler. You'd think it was holding and then it would crash down. They knew; their heads had been banged. So they waited until all was clear, until they were sure, until my "Load up" command, to scamper into the bed of the truck. They pirouetted as I threw in the special bright orange trash bags that the waste station required and slid in the red recycling bins of bottles, cans, and paper. They stuck their heads through the open sliding-glass window between the cab and the camper as I drove the truck out the drive.

The dogs were right; it was a thrill to drive the truck, the radio station rocking, the rugged-terrain tires bouncing over the asphalt patches in the road, making the bottles and cans clatter and clink. Under the shady canopy of the trees that arched over the curvy road, the dogs rode noses against camper shell screens and ears blown back. The scent of pungent cow pastures and sweet, fresh-cut hay rushed past them.

Once we took the left turn onto Garrison Chapel Road and crossed the rise of the railroad tracks, I looked over my shoulder to the dogs and sang, "To the dump, to the dump, to the dump dump dump." You know, the *Lone Ranger* theme song, which some prefer to call the *William Tell Overture,* which goes with the joke "Where does the Lone Ranger take his trash?" It was Emily's childhood joke, morphed into dog tradition.

The white-haired guy at the waste station liked the girls. He waited for me to open, balance, and jam-support the camper shell door before helping me throw the big bags into the iron dumpsters and sort the steel from the aluminum cans. Digs ran over and schmoozed while Lila nervously jumped through the cab window into the front seat. The old guy was handsome in the same comfortable way my grandfather was. He wore jeans and a light blue denim work shirt that was always clean even though he worked with trash. His hair in a tidy tapered cut and his manner calm, he brought a straightforward virtue to the dump that surely discouraged many from sneaking in forbidden items such as Styrofoam peanuts or cans of used paint. His emanating honesty and kindness must have made some save batteries for the recycling container and not hide used motor oil in their trash. He remembered everyone who came to the dump. He knew this truck and these dogs from the years when the dump run had been Jim's chore. But he didn't remember it was my truck, and he didn't remember Jim was dead.

"Whatever happened to your dad?" He asked me this question on a regular basis. "He's the one who used to come."

"He died," I said, politely not correcting his mistake, sadly remembering how sharply surgery, chemo, and cancer had aged Jim, and trying to ignore the image of Jim's last look that appeared in front of me.

Then, as always, he knit his smooth brow and remembered. "Oh, yes. Are you living out there by yourself now?"

Another question he'd asked dozens of times. I closed the back of the truck and answered, as always, "No, the dogs live there too." I waved good-bye as we drove out of the gravel lot, heading toward town and Burger King.

This was the dog's highlight of the dump run. Coming into town, the traffic building, a little barking at motorcycles and noisy cars, the smoky smell of the flame broiler growing closer, working our way through the strip mall, pulling into a parking place, waiting for me to return with a lumpy paper sack with two cheeseburgers inside.

I opened the driver's side door to find two black dog heads, chins sitting on the edge of the rear pass-through window. Eyes darting between me and the paper sack. "Ummmmmm," I said. "Cheeeeeeseburgas." Slowly I opened the bag and brought one burger out, a small package wrapped in paper marked *Plain*. One flap, two flap, three flaps, four flaps open. The slightly smashed and torn bun, small flat slab of ground beef not even a quarter of an inch thick, and gooey orange cheese sticking to the wrapper.

I scraped the cheese off the wrapper with my finger. "Ummm-mmm." I took a bite of the burger, demonstrating the excellence of the treat, good enough for humans. Eyes glued onto the motions of my hands. First torn-off bite goes to Lila, who is so greedy; the second to Digs, who is more polite and can wait.

I think the dogs love me from the moment I look toward the truck all the way to their first burger bites. But from that point forward, they resent my stinginess. *Why just two cheeseburgers? Why not double cheeseburgers? Why just once a month? Why do you have to take a bite? You can get one any time. Why do you get to decide who gets the first bite?*

It's a myth that dogs give unconditional goo-goo love, that they are the very epitome of loyalty. Anyone who pays attention knows that dogs have agendas and conditions. Negotiations and deception are involved on both sides of the species.

Shelter dogs come with a complicated set of expectations, and my sweet pound cakes are no exception. Lila expects that sooner or later someone will try to kill her or beat her. She loves me as hard as any dog has, and I think she is grateful for being saved from the evil world before Dog Paradise but deep down wouldn't be surprised if someday I turned violent, for that's been her experience with humans. Her overall advice is to choose your friends carefully, especially men, and be alert for the slightest change in the wind.

Digs agrees that humans are unreliable, but in a different way. She thinks they promise and then renege. From the puppy way she plays and her attraction to boys around age ten, I think she spent her early days as a kid's dog, believing life would be full of fun. And then something went wrong. She was about two years old when she was picked up by animal control for fornicating on a corner like a naughty tattooed slut hanging out with bad boys drinking beer and smoking cigarettes. Her family never called or retrieved her from the shelter.

Jim and I got the girls together at the shelter the first year we owned the house. It was shortly after the death of my good dog Samuel, for whom Dog Paradise had originally been constructed. Jim's dog had died a few months earlier. I didn't like being alone in the country with no neighbors, and since Jim wasn't moving in until the workshop was done "in the fullness of time," we decided to get another generation of dogs. Like buying the house, it was a new thing for us to do jointly. Diggity was Jim's dog, named for the old Perry Como song *Hot Diggity (Dog Ziggity Boom)*, because she danced and pranced around, ready to party at the drop of a hat. Most people thought she was named for digging in the yard. She was good at that too.

After we were approved by the shelter, after the dogs were spayed and Digs had her abortion, Jim didn't want her. "You keep both of them," Jim had said. "Train them together and give me Diggity when you're done. I don't have the patience for it anymore."

So poor Digs thought she was my dog. The pair of them was a handful. Untutored and wild. Not a single notion of civility between them. So I took Lila and Digs to obedience school – hand-signal and phrase-trained them the basics. Sit, stay, down, come, load up, heel, place, out, walk, go for a ride. And Diggity was a sweetheart to me until the day Jim decided to take her back.

But to screw around with me, Jim refused to use any of the words Diggity had learned. "I don't believe in training," he said as if he had never trained dogs to balance treats on their noses, cats to retrieve pennies, or me to stick around. "If a dog doesn't know what you want it to do, what damned good is it?" This pissed off Digs. She'd look at me, pleading for assistance with him, and I would turn away because I knew she was going to have to handle him herself. I knew that in the end she would love Jim more than me, that her life would be full of rides in the truck, constant companionship, games, and excellent snacks. But she believed I had betrayed her. She had trustingly transferred her affection to me, and I gave her away.

It turned out I was wrong about Diggity falling in love with Jim. He never fully bonded with her, and she developed a stress displacement habit of digging at the floor with her forepaws whenever she was petted. Then she was shunned while Jim was sick, turned into an outdoor dog who watched Jim die through the bedroom window, and ended up with me as her owner again. She didn't trust me. If we were going on a trash-and-burger run or heading into the woods for a walk, she was cheerful and happy. That's because I was doing what she wanted me to do. She would shallowly flirt with strangers, especially men, for a scratch behind the ear or the toss of a ball, but her heart was steeled up. Sometimes I caught her looking at me with her hard, foxy eyes and sensed that she hated me. Not because I beat her or wanted to kill her, but because I didn't love her properly.

And it was hard to love Diggity, or even like her. Since Jim's death, she had developed into a very anxious dog that shed excessively. Adding to her floor-digging obsession, she jumped up on guests, ignored my commands to sit or stay (she had unlearned them, thanks to Jim), and no longer asked to go out to use the bathroom (a real problem since she had also developed nervous, runny bowels). She was horribly jealous of Lila, snapping at her and pushing her way between us.

She was so overwrought. The Dog Whisperer would tell me that I needed to project a calm-assertive, pack-leader energy. True enough, but I knew that she had the buzz, the same buzz that I'd had. That she likely got it from me and my buzzy energy. Who knows? Maybe she saw Jim's last look float up when least expected too.

I reached through the rear window of the truck cab to place a calm-assertive hand on Digs's head. She nervously wriggled under my touch, wildly licked my hand, and compulsively dug at the bed of the pickup. We had a long way to go before she trusted that any calm-assertive action on my part was reliable and stable.

The best I could do in the In Between was go on with our day. I threw the truck into reverse and headed to the Square to hunt for a free parking space. I tried to find a shady spot away from a busy sidewalk, hoping to minimize any oh so politically incorrect barking at innocent sidewalk pedestrians who might mull over calling the police about the bad, savage country dogs left to bake in the back of the truck.

Eager to find out the truth about the septic system, I bounded up the steps of the beaux-artsy, flat-faced limestone building that used to serve as the city's post office back in 1911 and took my place in the requisite line that forms in any bureaucratic setting. I got a mystery-flavor Dum Dum pop from the free candy basket on the counter and read the poster about not dumping anything down storm drains that you wouldn't drink.

"I can't find those files," said the clerk when my turn came, with an administrative shake of her head.

"But I called ahead. Copies are supposed to be waiting for me," I said in a calm-assertive tone.

She scooted her glasses back and sighed. "Who did you talk to?"

I explained my several calls and watched her eyes squint and jaw set as she listened. "Just a minute," she said. She walked into the back and returned with a few sheets of paper, shaking her head. "He pulled out the file but didn't tell me."

I soon pushed out the double glass doors of the building with a promise of septic certainty in my hand, headed for coffee at the Scholars Inn Bakehouse café just a block away.

Carole was on the edge of her chair, texting, head bent to the black phone in her hand. She looked up as I drew out the chair across from her. "Look, it's the plan for my septic system," I boasted. "Now I'll know what's out there."

Flipping back the pages, I couldn't believe what I saw. The official diagram looked like my terrible hand sketch, but worse, with no dimensions or reference points to the rest of the property.

"Have you been having trouble with your septic?" Carole asked as she tried to follow my agitated pointing and page turning.

"No. There's just something I don't understand. I was sure the approval records of the system replacement would show where the fingers of the field were. But I was wrong; this is like a bad, shitty joke."

"I get it," Carole said drily, as I got up to get my coffee.

At the milk and sugar station a strong-chinned guy in a tight black T-shirt stirred milk into his eco-cool paper coffee cup as his languid sensuality drew half-lidded glances from a wide radius of women, including me. I wondered if he was the walking wounded, like Digs, with angry red welts on his heart, or if he was secure in his love status, like Carole was with her husband. They had this palpable groove. From my distant perch they seem to have a charmed life, despite trouble and accidents I'd heard only tidbits about. Both gregarious, both good-looking. Successful careers. Supportive families. Bighearted. Resilient. Smart. And never once acting superior, as some coupled people do, never holding me with my nebulous status in the world of love at arm's length like a stinky rag.

I refocused to listen to Carole. Her father was dying, and her mother was sick in Indianapolis; her many brothers and sisters were struggling with one another as they coped. Carole and her husband were retired, but he couldn't seem to stay retired and had been lured back to work by state government reformers. She was straddling life between their Indianapolis condo and their house out by the lake, between life and death, between old and new. Yet in what could have been a litany flushed with complaint, her tone was smooth, and she stopped from time to time to linger lightly on a little point of irony.

Carole got up for more coffee.

The hunk in the T-shirt had disappeared. Out the window, the golden yellow reblooming daylilies of the Vietnam Vets Memorial glowed in the midday sun.

My mind drifted to a lunch conversation I'd had a couple summers ago with an old friend I rarely see anymore, one of several friendships that shriveled after Jim died.

"I tell you," she'd said, "I have had it. He calls at eight last night to say he's on the way home, but he doesn't show up until eleven-thirty. I have dinner waiting, I'm starving, I think I hear him a million times coming up the drive. I don't know why I bother. Then when he gets home, smelling like a brewery, he lays into me for being pissed. Says I'm hemming him in and he needs room. If I hadn't had dinner ready, he would have gotten into a snit for that too. He said he just stopped in down the road to see if our neighbor had gotten her window fixed. If I know him, he was wanting something else fixed. He says I'm ridiculous to be jealous, but I know he's slept with every woman between here and town that he can. He denies it, but I know it's true."

As always, I had callously reminded her of the truth. Her husband had been coming home late for years, so what's new? Instead of understanding that she wanted a reality that had never been hers – a pleasant dinner every night with her honey – I had asked her why she didn't just fix dinner for herself and let him fend for himself when he got home.

"Why don't you just leave him if it's so bad?" I had said. "Do what you want. Forget about what he does. Quit trying to change him."

Shut down by my insensitivity, she had stabbed at her food and said, "Oh, I dunno."

I had been so tired of this whiny conversation. We'd been having it for years. Sometimes it was reversed, me explaining why I wasn't breaking things off with Jim because deep down, despite how complicated and difficult our relationship was, we were connected.

Jim and I didn't have a smooth groove like Carole had with her husband, but we did have a groove.

When I got home I walked out to the lawn on the other side of the blue spruce in front of the house, trying to imagine the location of the septic field and pipes. I looked at the papers from the health department, incredulous that this sketch would pass for a plan. I would have to guess, and wondered what the probability was of guessing correctly. I wasn't good at figuring odds.

*   *   *

I used to wonder what my chances were to ever have a long-term relationship, and my desire for one came and went like summer and winter, alternately influenced by social pressure that the only good way to be is coupled or married and my need to be in charge of my own life.

I am not alone in this. About a third of baby boomers are divorced, separated, or have never been married – and divorce is on the uptick as some, especially women, are tossing *till death do us part* out the same window they tossed their girdles. Love and relationships are as mysterious to me as my septic system was.

My first, hippie marriage, to Emily's dad, lasted a brief three years, one of which we spent separated. He thought we would become one, but I needed a strong breeze between us and finally a divide. Immediately following the end of that marriage, Emily and I lived with an adventurer/pipeliner/cabin-builder in Alaska for two contentious years. We were ill-suited, and he wanted to send Emily off to boarding school. It was this affair that inspired me to go back to college so that I could quit depending on men for income and gain control over my life. Once I got going in my career, I had a lurching, long-distance affair with a rich, married executive for two years. He taught me how to eat lox and bagels in bed while reading the *New York Times,* drink expensive brandy, and be deceived by a man with a stable of lovers.

I liked being independent and loved the freedom that my relationship with Jim gave me: the freedom to come and go as I pleased, buy or sell whatever I wanted without asking, to not cook dinner or talk to anyone after a hard day at work. We used to say we were volunteers. *The door is always open; if you are here it's because you want to be.* I think that open door helped both of us stick around, because we didn't feel restrained or boxed in.

Ours was no fairy-tale relationship. There would never be a newspaper article about us like the one I read the other day about an elderly couple who died within two days of each other after a gazillion years of marriage: "The two of them were completely intertwined," said a friend of the dead couple. "You couldn't tell where one stopped and the other started."

I don't mind that some people want or need to merge into one, breathe together, and walk in unison. But I do mind that those relationships are glorified and held up as better than all other ways of living as if that's the only good kind of love. As if inseparable, nonstop matrimony is the only way to live a happy life. I mind it that a single woman is seen culturally as a failure. That the hundreds of other ways to interact intimately with another person are dismissed as lesser forms of love.

In reality, only half of adults in the United States are married, and 30 percent live alone. And they aren't boo-hooing about it. In big cities like Manhattan, London, and Paris, the numbers spike up to 50 or 60 percent. That's not to say there aren't people out there who want a traditional relationship; I just don't think we all have to be slathered with it.

Still, in my world, the character of my relationship with Jim was constantly questioned and often labeled as insufficient. Even after he was dead, my boss termed it a marriage of convenience and deemed my grief nonexistent. Despite my clear and certain preference for our brand of open-air independence, I flinched when I felt the indictment of others. When things were rocky with Jim, I would bring forth Mr. Imaginary – the handsome, sexy, smart, witty, well-spoken, ambitious, charming, and (of course) independent guy who had yet to show up.

Mostly Jim and I were happy with each other, always secure in our friendship if not in our lover status. I fell in and out of love with Jim a few times over the years but was more in love than out. As surely as the seasons follow each other, Jim had bitter and dark periods, and I would let things ride and begin to think about putting him back on friends-without-benefits status. Just because we had some kind of undeniable deep connection didn't mean we had to be lovers. Then he would sense my withdrawal and muster a return from his black places. I would forget Mr. Imaginary, and we would meander on.

I never expected that Jim would say he loved me or that he would be an easy man to love. I liked a challenging man; my father was one. I myself am a difficult woman to love. And Jim came with a reputation as an emotionally remote, confirmed bachelor who lived first in his mother's house while she worked and lived out of town and, even worse, with her after she retired to Bloomington.

He held things close to the chest. Over the years, fragments of his story eventually floated to the surface. His was a brutal cross-generational tale of love, trust, and hope, all promised and snatched away. The great-great-uncle on his father's side gambled away the family fortune and their hard-earned northern Indiana farmlands. His grandmother on his mother's side was born in a well-to-do family. She married a forbidden handyman from their farm. The photo of her hung in the hallway of his family home, showing a classic dark-haired, impish Irish beauty in a high-collared white blouse, wearing a man's bowler hat and looking directly at the camera. She died in the 1918 influenza epidemic; her husband was maimed in an accident. The children were sent off to live with relatives. Jim's mom ended up with her father's mean, poor brother who mourned the death of his fair-haired daughter, also lost to influenza. Alone of her siblings, Jim's mom was denied a college education due to the foster family's inadequate funds. With her snapping Irish eyes, she made her way in the world as an independent woman, her backbone stiff, as one of the first female managers at the phone company. Maybe this is why Jim had been drawn to my independent ways.

It was always hard for me to imagine, but she once was loose and happy, playing piano and singing in a swing band. She caught the eye of a handsome World War II pilot who convinced her to marry on his leave. He immediately took off for Northern Africa. She was pregnant with Jim. Two more leaves, two more babies. And then the deepest betrayal.

The story goes like this: Finally the war was over, the family was together in northern Indiana; the dashing soldier now had a promising Goshen real estate business and his own airplane. One day he wanted to fly to a conference. The weather was foggy. There was an argument. He lied – promising to drive, not fly. His plane slammed into a shrouded tree. Three fatherless children. The eternal taste of deceit. Jim was six years old. The last photo before his world was permanently ruined shows a happy Jim in his cowboy outfit at Christmas, hair slicked back movie-cowboy Gene Autry style (giving his song *Ghost Riders in the Sky* a new, dark meaning). Jim was given the job of being the man of the family. After his father's death, his mother drew a curtain around herself and her children, and it became the four of them against the untrustworthy world, forever. Diggity would agree.

All the kids were notably clever but wary of happiness and unable to easily navigate relationships outside the family. One sister hanged herself while still in college on the other sister's birthday. Jim was taken under the wing by the local veterinarian and later admitted to Purdue University's rigorous College of Veterinary Medicine. Resentful that his life had been predetermined and sure he was ill-suited for the social demands required of a veterinarian (talking to people about their animals), he dropped out to join the marines for adventure. He came back carrying the load of his dead buddies, the DNA of his cells altered by Agent Orange. The world had confirmed that it cannot be trusted.

But I always thought that Jim did love me; he just didn't believe in saying it. "I don't even know what it means," he used to say. "I see people pledging love forever and then a few months or years later getting divorced."

And I was fine with that logic but looser with my own words of love. I believed serial monogamy was a fine approach and still loved my ex-husband and ex-Alaska lover – without wanting to be intimate. I loved Emily. I loved my cat and dogs. Sometimes I loved jobs or clients or projects. I loved fresh sliced tomatoes, sweet peonies, and the ever changing blues of the sky. Deep snow and the subtlety of the winter woods. I loved many friends, new and old. I loved my brother and sister. I loved Jim. Love was Jim's issue, not mine, or so I thought.

Jim's journals, the ones I'd found in the box above the workshop, were surprising to me in how rarely I was mentioned and revealing in his last entry, a few days after the death of his mother. There being "no reason to continue living now that she was dead," he had written. His words stung postmortem. What had I been to him, chopped liver?

Those had been grim times. When Jim's mother died, Jim banned me from the funeral, even though I'd been fully involved in her care and final days in the hospital. "It's for family only," he'd cruelly said as he slipped into a four-year melancholia. I was on the edge of moving away to Ohio for a new job when he rallied and convinced me to continue on with him and buy this house together. This house that refused to be sold.

Then he proceeded to work on breaking my heart. He didn't move in for two and a half long, embarrassing years, during which I tried to understand his reluctance or perhaps inability to make the move and commitment. It took getting married for me to become convinced that he didn't love me.

"It doesn't mean anything," he'd said caustically when he agreed to the idea of getting married so that I could retire early with health insurance. "We're only doing it for the insurance. I don't want anyone to know. Nothing will change. Everything I have goes to my sister."

I liked the idea of keeping our finances independent but was hurt at his pointed tone and insistence on secrecy. Was he ashamed to be married to me? Embarrassed to have lost his bachelor status? I wanted to add it to the List of Complaints, but it was too real.

A few days later I excused myself from a client meeting to meet Jim at the county clerk's office to tie our knot. She wanted us to have some vows.

"What do we need vows for?" said Jim. "This is just for the insurance; it means absolutely nothing." The clerk, accustomed to vowless couples, picked one from a collection in a three-ring binder. I don't remember what we said.

You might think that a self-determining, independent woman like me would have stopped at this point and chucked not only this marriage but this cruel man as well. But that would be making things too simple. For you see, I understood harsh love and maybe even liked it.

I was a daddy's girl when I was young. My father was fierce and brilliant, demanding and fascinating. A commanding figure with jet-black hair and a flashing white smile. A self-made, hungry man. He judged severely and parceled out his love stingily. At his knee I developed a taste for demanding, clever men who withheld affection. Mix that up with my undeniable attraction to sexy, adventuresome, bad-boy rebel irreverence, and my relationship with Jim was perfect.

Our connection went beyond romance. We had a deep link between us, that gold cord. Once, during a reconciliation, when Jim was convincing me to move from being friends with benefits to exclusive lovers, I worried that taking that step might ruin our friendship. Wisely, he told me that no matter what, we would always be friends.

It was true. We were authentic with each other. Yes, we lied and kept secrets about certain things, but mostly the curtains were open; the unwieldy truth about who we were was unvarnished. He, like no one else, knew the real me. He, like no one else, was cool with all of my inconsistencies, rightly calling me a chameleon. It's not like I'm particularly sweet and easy to love either.

And let's not forget the erotic edge of danger that comes with the risk of loving a difficult, smart man. Jim was the forbidden, the dangerous, the can't-be-explained. He was cruel, but he was also breathtakingly charming and engaging. I felt powerful because I could handle him, hold his attention, when all other women could not. I loved him. It might hurt, but it hurt so good.

People rarely talk about this kind of love. If they do, they dismissively call it abusive. As if this kind of relationship has less value or place in the world than the gooey ones. But I couldn't have a gooey, Hollywood romance with sweet, reliable love. I needed verve and uncertainty to stay interested.

Jim and I didn't get together to raise a family. Even though he adored Emily, we didn't get around to an exclusive relationship until after she graduated from high school. We never thought we were building a traditional partnership. We were attracted to each other for the challenge of it. For the tang of the bitter against the sweet.

I agreed that we didn't need to pledge love to each other, that we didn't need the hand of government or of God to stay together, but his mean-spirited repetition of "it means absolutely nothing" burrowed inside me. For us, marriage was not an indicator of the state of our relationship, but his comment seemed a needless cruelty that went beyond hallmark bad-boy indifference, and at the moment I married him I closed off my heart.

"It Means Absolutely Nothing" was noted in my gardening journal along with other new starts, all of which sooner or later died:

3/6   Indoor start: Zinnia Profusion Cherry, Whirligig
3/8   Jim & I get married
3/13   Seeded back hill
3/28   Moved Russian sage to end of thyme strip

The marriage made it easy for me to be Jim's caregiver and advocate when he was sick. I didn't have to fight anyone in the medical system for the right to be there. But that's all It Means Absolutely Nothing meant, or so I thought.

On our first and only anniversary (between chemo and brain surgery) of It Means Absolutely Nothing, Jim gave me a tiny gift-wrapped box. I was furious.

Over the years, Jim had held steady in anti–holiday gift giving (it was anti-commercialism rebellion that I understood – he was generous off-holiday). I liked holidays, so I would give him Christmas presents and bake him birthday cakes (which he loved). He violated his ethics for my fiftieth birthday when he bought me a hot-air balloon ride, but he had never given me a package to unwrap until the It Means Absolutely Nothing anniversary.

If It Means Absolutely Nothing, why would we exchange presents? I hadn't gotten him anything.

I glared at Jim when I opened the box. "You said this means absolutely nothing, and I figured you meant it." Inside was a gold commemorative coin for the year of our marriage.

He had shrugged, smiled, and said, "I had to get my Little Wifey something."

Since his chemotherapy treatment I'd been finding notes addressed to "Little Wifey." And he would be lovey-dovey when he called me Little Wifey to my face. But I never took the bait. Never smiled at the nickname. Never made up one for him. All I could feel when I opened that box was a sour scoff.

I put the It Means Absolutely Nothing keepsake in my coin collection along with a flimsy aluminum token he'd given me years ago imprinted with hearts and two birds and the phrase *Love Is for the Birds*.

As Jim's illness had crawled by and he did so much to be sure I was taken care of after his death, after he was so sweet to me on our Nova Scotia vacation, my sucker heart rejuvenated, and I began to wonder if maybe he'd had a change of heart too and did love me. I also wondered if he was instead suffering from brain damage. I didn't stop to think that maybe he had simply acknowledged me as family.

On the day he died, after his sister left but before his last big convulsion, I'd whispered in his ear, "I love you more than anything." And I did.

"And I love being loved by you," he replied.

At least he didn't lie to me.

*   *   *

A week or so after Jim died, one of his old girlfriends called me in the middle of the night. "I wanted you to know that Jim loved you," she'd drunkenly said as I listened in a raggedy bad mood. "He told me he did."

What? He confesses love of me to her, but not to me?

I told Emily about this.

"Oh, Momma," she said without hesitation. "He was just like Harrison Ford in *The Empire Strikes Back*. Han Solo couldn't tell Princess Leia he loved her either. It would be out of character."

Maybe Jim was like bad-boy Han Solo and loved me but couldn't say it. Maybe he didn't love me. Or maybe both. I could only guess. But the truth was that I would never know and that it didn't make a bit of difference anymore, 'cause the guy I'd been with had up and split.

14

Fumes

The blocky woman stuck out her hip between the man I was watching and the row of wooden baskets. He smiled and stepped back to give her room. She solidly established her squat body in front of the bushel of small sweet onions. He had already given way to a determined woman with a huge baby stroller, her clay face puffy beneath the eyes from lack of sleep. But he wasn't impatient; he simply let the moments stretch. Maybe he loved the push and shove of these women shoppers, their own barely discernible pungent smell a good companion for onions.

Still, you could tell he wanted his turn at the onions. I had been watching him for a while from my sideline seat on the curb. I waved a distant hello at a woman I'd met in the writing class and lazily swung my view around the farmer's market, a Saturday event that was partly about vegetables and mostly about Bloomington's social scene. It was in high style on the sultry morning I stood watching the onion shoppers. The market was full of the August harvest of Flamin' Fury and Redhaven peaches, Brandywine and Mortgage Lifter tomatoes, Red Knight and Early Sunsation bell peppers, Silver Queen and Ambrosia sweet corn, and Swedish Peanut Fingerling and Adirondack Blue potatoes.

Fiddle cases were open for shoppers' dollars; musicians leaned together intertwining bluegrass harmonies. My toes tapped as I hummed along to "The Banks of the Ohio": *And only say that you'll be mine / In no others' arms entwine.*

The lusty bounty of produce stimulated the display of university town eccentricities like peacocks fan their tails. There was the spectacle of footwear – sandals with purple polyester webbing, black ballerina flats printed with pairs of red cherries, and curry-colored cloth loafers. And the earring exhibition – dangling, layered metal shapes, tiny orbs of glass and stone, silver studs and loops in lips and ears and noses and belly buttons. The competitive collection of sisal woven bags, straw baskets from Africa, and canvas totes slung over shoulders – pink and lime polka dots, swirly geo-prints, and orange and green stripes.

The guy in the onion line caught my eye again as he shifted his gaze to a woman at the nearby egg stand. There a young man laughed lightly as he gave her change for a dozen pricey blue and green Ameraucana eggs. She was a willowy woman in orange print capris, low on the hips. Midnight blue Celtic-knot tattoos angled along her shoulder under the thin, black straps of her tank top. Wisps of maroon hair played along the long curve of her neck, her moist skin translucent, shimmering in the early morning light.

Necks, I love necks. I used to kid Jim, saying, "I don't really like you; I just love the way your neck smells. Every time I think about leaving you, all I have to do is smell your neck and all is good." I remembered running my nose along his clavicle to his neck, inhaling him, down the edge of his jaw, falling into a long, soft kiss.

More quickly than I would have thought, I had found myself drawn to the idea of finding another companion. It started unexpectedly the fall after Jim died. I missed being touched, having someone to pal around with, enjoying a familiar conversation style. I thought another guy would be the answer.

I was a difficult date when I was young and sexy – shifting, unpredictable, argumentative, not vulnerable enough. I figured I had even poorer chances now that I'd matured into my full, opinionated self. Actually, there was little chance of my even getting a date. Statistics show that only 8 percent of widows age fifty-five to sixty-four remarry, and less than 2 percent do after that. It didn't occur to me that maybe the women of these demographics didn't want to remarry. That they found touch, companionship, and conversation in a different way.

Right around Thanksgiving, after dancing solo at Emily's wedding, I plunked down almost two hundred dollars for a six-month subscription to the online dating site eHarmony. "Get matched with men that are compatible with you in important characteristics such as core values, sense of humor, and character with our Scientifically Proven Compatibility Matching System." I carefully answered their 436 questions about 29 compatibility dimensions. The results said I believed deeply in personal freedom and individual responsibility, embraced all of life's emotions, was both disciplined and a free spirit. That I was an introvert. Sound like a fun date?

I thought this would be a good time for Mr. Imaginary to show up. As smart as Jim, still a ravishing reader, but more social, less of a recluse, with just a hint of bad boy. Maybe a natty dresser, maybe someone connected to the university, maybe someone who would dance with me. I imagined dinners in houses full of art and books, conversations with other couples about a play we'd all just seen, the colors bronze and copper green, undulating rhythms of global music quietly moving through our bodies as we sipped wine from big-globed glasses.

I imagined him next to me as we wandered through the market, nodding at other couples and confirming plans for the next gathering. I saw us trundling off to have a post-market lunch downtown, followed by working in the yard together, and later listening and laughing as Guy Noir, private eye, tried to find the answers to life's persistent questions on *Prairie Home Companion.* Or cooking dinner together, chopping and stirring and tasting while filling the air with Machu Picchu vacation plans.

Immediately I got a match with a guy from Bloomington. His photos showed a lean, nerdy, gray-haired, slope-shouldered man in running shorts. I reminded myself to be open-minded – after all, if this had been a sixty-five-year-old Jim, he wouldn't look so buff either.

It took two days of email for him to ask how much I liked sex.

"I need someone who enjoys frequent hugs and kisses who likes to hold hands and have frequent physical, tactile touching, a physical connectivity," he wrote. "There is more to a mutually enjoyable sexual relationship than simply intercourse in the missionary position. If you are very sexually conservative we probably wouldn't do well."

This was modern dating? Before he even knew my last name, before we met in person, he asked if I'd do it in any other position besides the missionary one.

How unsavory. How unsexy. I told him I was no prude and dumped him for bad decision making. I soon discovered that it's hard to find a match within three hundred miles on eHarmony, and I wanted to shop locally just like I did for my vegetables. But this fruitless exchange about sex gave me plenty to think about.

Figuring out if someone likes sex is a big topic in eHarmony. You can ask how important chemistry is or how romantic or physically affectionate someone is. You can make "willing to explore our sexual desires with passion and understanding" a Must Have.

I was confounded about how to answer questions about chemistry or the role of sex in my relationship. Sex had been a seamless part of my relationship with Jim. There were times when we inhaled each other like pure cocaine, but for us sex was always connected to the frontal lobe and our spicy confrontational exchanges.

After Jim had his prostate removed, sex became more elusive and dependent upon self-injected vasodilator drugs. "It's time for small injections," we'd say in low husky tones, trying to knock off the clinical coldness of unwrapping needles to stick into his tender tissues.

Toward the end we hoarded the drugs, worried he would die before getting more if we used them up; saving them meant he would stay alive. I threw the remaining one away along with the hospice drugs.

"You got me hotter than Georgia asphalt," I had whispered in his ear the last time we had small injections. It was Lula's line to Sailor in David Lynch's nicely deviant movie *Wild at Heart*. A lie, of course, but why not a sweet lie among the harsh truths of cancer?

Our affection and intimacy peaked right before he died, when sex wasn't even in the room with us. You can't get any more intimate than caring for your dying lover.

So how am I supposed to answer the question, "How important is sexual chemistry?" It's a stupid online-dating question, because you don't have a choice and mostly are not even aware of what's going on. On a biological level, chemistry is the invisible guide through life. Pheromones set off all kinds of behavioral responses. Not only are they aphrodisiacs, but they can also trigger flight in aphids when attacked and aggression in bees when harassed. Ants use them to mark food trails. Dogs have them in urine to mark territory. The acacia tree repels giraffes browsing by increasing bitter tannin in its leaves, and it sends out pheromone alarm signals. In response, neighboring trees raise tannin levels too.

All mammals have a nasogenital alliance, a fumy pathway of nerves and neurotransmitters linking the olfactory membrane in the nose to the genitalia. Some people insist that pheromones orchestrate groups of women to menstruate on the same cycle. Others claim that underarm sweat pheromone compounds added to perfume improves the likelihood of getting laid. Some research points to our ability to sense immune system genes, preferring those different from ours, and that straight men and women smell different from gays. Whatever the truth, there's something going on beneath our consciousness that is so primitive we certainly couldn't fill out a questionnaire about it.

This spring, statistics be damned, I began to suddenly attract men. Maybe I was pumping out pheromones, because men began to hover around me like fruit flies take to ripe tomatoes.

It started one night when I ran into an old acquaintance, a man I had briefly dated before I met Jim. He was sort of a haunted Walter Matthau/Jeff Goldblum mix. I had been persuaded by friends to go out to the Player's Pub bar to see a local band. After a couple of two-dollar bottles of Rolling Rock, I found myself dancing with him to the love potion blues of Carlyn Lindsey and Snake Doctor. He was cool and suave in his loose, tropical shirt.

Against a mean piano, the band's Janis Joplinesque singer belted out an apt tune.

But on the other hand
Talk is cheap
I'm awful new on my own
Maybe I'll decide to get a good night's sleep
Or maybe I should follow you home.

Toward the end of the night, he asked, "Would you try ballroom dancing with me? Go to a Party Night at Arthur Murray? It's for newcomers. That's where I take lessons. They play music and serve wine."

Remembering my smooth, fox-trotting father and thrilled by the occasional touch of Mr. Matthau/Goldblum's hand, I said, "Okay."

He smiled broadly. "I'll meet you there on Wednesday evening."

I was a little late on Wednesday. While driving into town, I suddenly wondered if I'd put on deodorant. I couldn't remember. I always do, but what if I'd forgotten? I stopped at a drugstore on the way and then pulled into the Eastland Plaza strip mall parking lot. The neon sign glowed in the window of the narrow, dimly lit dance studio between a big-chain pet store and a tropical tanning salon. I could see Mr. Matthau/Goldblum waiting inside the front door while I smeared the roll-on under my arms in the restricted space under my shirt.

"There you are!" he said, looking nervously at his watch and sliding a clipboard my way when I finally pushed open the glass door. "Sign your name on this sheet. Put me down as your referral. It gives me dance credits."

Hand on my elbow, he quickly steered me to the back room. A line of beige folding chairs ran the length of one wall.

"It feels a little like eighth-grade dance lessons," I said as I picked up a plastic cup with a meager splash of wine from a table by the door. I wondered if it would be bad form to go back for seconds.

"It will be fun. You'll see."

We sat in the middle of the line of chairs. Directly in front of us was an unavoidable floor-to-ceiling mirror across the length of the whole room. There, reflected back, was an almost unrecognizable dumpy woman looking distressed, in low-heeled old-lady shoes.

Someone started a CD. Guitar chords. *DO, do DOOT.* The Rolling Stones.

Mr. Matthau/Goldblum said, "We do the swing to this."

The swing? Isn't the swing for Glenn Miller?

"Okay," I said gamely, putting my hand into his and feeling his touch at the small of my back.

"It's easy. Step, step, rock, step."

At the beginning of each new song, Mr. Matthau/Goldblum would cock his head, listen to a few beats, and then start a waltz, foxtrot, salsa, Lindy hop, merengue, or cha-cha while I stumbled around. I vaguely remembered the basics from dance classes. I already knew the box step, and all of these dances seemed derivations of that. But knowing the steps didn't help the awkwardness. I tried to breathe, but it seemed as if the air around us was oxygen-deprived, as if the space between us was full of hidden yellow jackets that would swarm out if our bodies accidently touched.

The lights switched on. The instructor announced upcoming dance lesson specials. I gathered my purse from the floor by the chairs. The balls of my feet were tender and burning.

"How often do you come here to dance?" I asked Mr. Matthau/Goldblum.

"Almost every night. I'll show you my dance history."

I followed him to the front counter, where he asked for his binder.

"Look, this is my progress." He put a loose-leaf notebook in my hands. "You can move up to bronze, silver, or gold levels. I like to go up to Indianapolis for dance competitions; some people compete nationally. I've been dancing here for over a year. I love it; it's so much fun. It makes me feel good about myself. Maybe you'd like it. You could start taking lessons too, two or three nights a week."

I looked through the menu of dance lessons and the respective prices. This could run into hundreds of dollars.

"I'll think about it," I said, knowing my spreadsheet couldn't handle this expense.

His phone beeped with a text message. "Let's go meet my friends for a drink. They're over at TGI Friday's at the mall right now."

I'm not a mall person. I hate malls. I don't like the stale smells, the long corridors of things I don't want. I abhor the dullness of mass chain-store mentality. I would never go to TGI Friday's on my own.

"Okay, sure," I said, thinking about the need to be open-minded.

We drove separately. Inside the restaurant it was standard freezing-air-conditioning cold. The smell of burgers and fries hit my nose. Mr. Matthau/Goldblum headed over to a tall table where two people sat. I slid into one of the high bar chairs.

He introduced me: "She tried out Party Night."

He introduced them: "This is my dance crowd."

They nodded, giving me a quick appraisal. He flowed toward his friends like water as he ordered a scotch. Soon they broke into in-crowd chatter. His iPhone on order. His Mac computer. Photo editing programs they were using. Technology philosophies. The old days when they lived in New York City, where their kids lived now. I was good with technology; I'd been to New York. I tried to dart into the conversation here and there, but I could tell by the tightening of their faces at each of my interjections that I was somehow off-kilter. The easy comfort they had together seemed frozen to me, like the ice in my gin and tonic.

Afterward, in the stark amber ring of a parking lot light, we faced each other stiffly. Still cold in the spring night air, I wrapped my arms around myself. Mr. Matthau/Goldblum briefly and safely hugged me over my folded arms. I could feel the warmth of his body; his touch melted a small spot in my tension. It made me brave.

"Why don't you give me a call? We could get to know each other better," I said.

"Do you want to go sailing this Sunday? I have a boat on the lake."

"Sure!" Sailing? Dancing and sailing? It all sounded so fun, although I was yet to have anything but fun.

The next day around noon the phone rang. It was him.

"I need a dance partner for Latin Night on Saturday night. Would you like to come? What about dinner? We could have dinner. What do you like to eat? Where should we eat?"

"Anything but lima beans. How about that Afghan restaurant on the square?"

"I'll pick you up. Tell me where you live."

Dates! I had two dates. Dancing on Saturday night and sailing on Sunday.

On Saturday I tried on outfit after outfit in front of the mirror on the back of my bedroom door, clothes piling on the bed. Surely there was something that didn't emphasize my rolls, something with some swish, something that didn't make me look ridiculous. A black swing-hem skirt was the only choice, but it was too tight at the waist, squeezing pudgy rolls out into a classic muffin top. A loose, long, sparkly shirt might hide the bulges. Maybe he wouldn't notice. Or at least maybe I wouldn't be able to see it in the wall of mirror.

What about shoes? Not the stodgy T-straps. My closet was full of European-style clogs and Mary Janes. Not Latin Night at all. I'd given up on high heels when I quit my job, but I hadn't gotten rid of them all. Peep-toe pumps, fine leather sling-backs, and funky suede high heels. They were hanging in a shoe organizer on the back of the laundry room door in case I needed a pair for a funeral or a wedding. I scurried downstairs. *Oh, these little shoes with the rhinestone toe band and the clear heels.* I'd danced in them at Emily's wedding. I plucked them from their pocket, sat on the basement steps, kicked off my green suede clogs, pulled off my socks, and directed my toes down the silvery insoles. I could hardly squeeze my toes in. *How did I ever wear these shoes?* My feet, freed from narrow work shoes, had widened. I would have to wear the T-straps. Pretend they looked like dance shoes.

Just as the sun set blazing orange over the horse pasture across the road, Mr. Matthau/Goldblum pulled up in the drive, the dogs barking in alarm at his arrival. The mares kicked and flashed their tails. I watched him from the big front window as he got out of the car. He was handsome in a sleek, open-necked shirt.

He ran his eyes over me when I opened the door, a glimmer of disappointment flickering across his face. Tension solidified in my shoulders, a low gurgle threatened in my gut. I wanted to stay home, but instead I tucked myself into the passenger seat of his car.

We rode silently into town. My attempts at small talk – "How was your week? The weather looks good for tomorrow" – got one-word responses. We endured a stilted silence that followed us into the restaurant.

"What do you like?" I asked.

"I don't eat out much and don't know this menu. We'll have to hurry. There's not much time. Order something that will come fast."

Wordlessly we picked at our meals. His shoulders were hunched over, and his eyes looked anywhere but at me.

At the strip mall dance studio, the same dumpy woman appeared in the giant mirror. I set my purse down again by the line of chairs while Mr. Matthau/Goldblum pulled a pair of black, pointy-toed, soft leather dance shoes out of a bag he had carried in. He pushed his loafers under the chairs as a percussive instrumental filled the room.

I stood nervously.

He lightly placed his hand on my upper back and moved into the rhythm. "It's quick-quick slow, quick-quick slow."

Around me wiggled skintight red salsa dresses swaying in strappy high-heeled sandals that crossed over and dipped. I plastered on my best false grin and laughed nervously, trying hard not to look in the mirror. Mr. Matthau/Goldblum knew all the steps, but his gaze was glued to the ceiling, a pained look on his face. After a few cha-chas and sambas, he handed me over to a nearby dance instructor.

"Keep the top of your body still. Bend your knees. Your foot action will move your hips," the instructor said. I thought I felt the beginnings of a little groove, but he shortly deposited me in a chair to dance with another potential lesson taker. I joined the line of single women sitting in the chairs as couples sinuously rumbaed their way around the room.

The ten-mile ride back to my house in the country was long and silent. I wanted to find a way to puncture the tension. There was nothing between us. Where was that chemistry? Could I ignite it, make the heavy blackness between us sag away?

I opened the car door, and Mr. Matthau/Goldblum walked beside me to the house. The big at-the-door-moment hung in the night air.

"Could I touch your cheek?" I surprised myself by asking.

In the pool of light by the front door, his face flattened. His eyes darted to one side.

"Yes," he said in a dull voice.

Embarrassed that I had asked, wishing that my mouth had stayed shut, I ran the back of one finger across his cheek. He pulled back ever so slightly. Then he abruptly said, "I'll pick you up around noon tomorrow." As I turned to unlock the door he melted into the dark of the long driveway.

The next day was no better. First a long, tongue-tied drive out to the lake while Mr. Matthau/Goldblum's tiny dog barked and snapped at me. His small sailboat seemed almost bereft. Barren. A few musty cushions. He quickly set sail and then tacked back and forth at the edge of the harbor, sometimes in a circle, like an affair going nowhere. His black hair blew in the wind. He lifted his head to inhale the lake and then looked at me.

"I think I should tell you." The words rushed out of him. "I'm madly in love. It's with a married woman. She won't leave her husband. We don't have sex. But she fills my mind. It's probably hopeless, but I love everything about her."

"Oh." *Stupid. I am stupid.* What was it about his refusal to look at me or pulling back from my touch that didn't scream his lack of interest in me? No pheromones here.

"So I'm not looking for someone to date, but a friend, a dancing partner. Want to be friends?"

"Oh, sure. We can be friends. We are friends. We've known each other forever. Of course, friends. Dancing, sure. I'll take lessons." *Lies, lies. I didn't feel friendly.*

My chest was tight, my breathing shallow. My gut was gurgling. Uncomfortable, disconnected. I should have quit the whole thing after that first awful Party Night. Instead I had willingly tossed all my instincts and anti-high-heeled-shoe values right out the window, all because I was obsessed with being touched. What was wrong with me?

Tuesday afternoon, Mr. Matthau/Goldblum called.

"Would you like to go dancing?"

"No, I've decided it's just not me."

"Then we should do something else. Go hiking? You like to do that."

"Yeah, sure, maybe. But I'm busy this week. I've got a branding project to work on. Some other time." Not brave enough to walk away honestly.

When I hung up the phone, it startled me by ringing again. I let the answering machine screen the call to avoid Mr. Matthau/Goldblum, just in case he, like me, couldn't hear between the lines.

Meanwhile I went downstairs and put all of my high-heeled shoes in paper grocery sacks to take to Goodwill.

On the machine was a message from Jim's sister. She wanted to sell the Monte Carlo.

The black 1983 Chevy coupe with opera-style windows, a plush red interior, and checkered-flag hubcaps had belonged to Jim's mom. A potential muscle car. When I had transferred the car title from Jim's estate to his sister, I'd mentioned the brilliant idea of calling a James Deanish friend who had a souped-up black Buick; maybe he would want this classic car too.

I called her back. Our conversations were always sparse.

"Here's his number," I said, reading it off to her from the phone book.

For decades I'd had a forbidden smoldering uneasiness about this man. When we were young, he was dangerous. A bad, bad sexy boy with sparkling blue eyes who drank lots of whiskey and ingested who knows what drugs. I always had to step outside to catch my breath when Jim and I went to his house. I'd heard that he had cleaned up his act, was sober, maybe even organic.

"If he wants to look at the car, can you be here too? I don't know him."

"Okay, try for something next week."

In a tight, white T-shirt and jeans, Mr. James Dean walked slowly around the Monte Carlo parked in the driveway of Jim's family house, where his sister lived. His loose-jointed sexiness poured out as smooth as high-grade motor oil. He lifted the heavy black hood.

The smell of old grease yawned up while I leaned over the broad front fender, watching him pull out dip sticks and push on gaskets. "It's not in very good shape," he said, shaking his head. "This V8 has no horsepower. I don't think I want it."

"You want to drive it?" I asked, trying to keep my mind on the topic. "Give Jim's sister an idea of what it's worth?"

A slow, gorgeous smile. "Okay, why don't you come too?"

Jim's mother had quit driving the car several years before she died. He and I used to cruise around in it on summer Saturday nights. We'd join the line of teenagers in high-rise pickups and hot-rods with neon lights on the undercarriage that parades down the main street of Bloomington. I'd slide across the seat, and Jim would throw his arm over my shoulder as if I were sixteen. I'd roll his cigarette pack up in his T-shirt sleeve and smoke one for old times' sake.

"I wish I'd known you when I got out of the marines," he had often told me. "I would have pulled up in front of your house in my black GTO and honked the horn. You would have run out in your little plaid high school skirt, door slamming behind you, and jumped in. We would have peeled off down the street and never looked back."

When I slid into the Monte Carlo's familiar seat again, my brain started to steam and a rush of excitement raced from my throat to my knees like a Pavlovian dog. I rolled down the passenger-side window to blow away the slight mildew smell erupting from the noisy air conditioner as Mr. James Dean backed out of the driveway.

"With the weather warming up I've got my motorcycle back on the road," he said. "You ever interested in a ride? The back roads."

I felt my cheeks flush. "Oh, yeah, that would be great."

*   *   *

A few days later Mr. James Dean pulled up into my driveway on a slick-looking, angular motorcycle. The girls had never seen anything like it. He didn't have a helmet on, and he hadn't brought one for me.

An illicit thrill ran through me as I settled in behind him, leaning forward into a racy riding position. As he zipped out the drive, my legs gripped around him and I felt my tits press flat against his muscular back. I couldn't hear the dogs barking over the revving, and torquing, and clutching. Our bodies leaned into the curves of Harmony Road. The wind rushed through my hair as we shot past Kirksville and then caught Popcorn Road cross-country to pull into the parking lot of the Lake Monroe dam.

I stretched my shaky legs, hoping he wouldn't notice that it took a few steps for my right old-lady hip to work well. We walked the gravel path to the lake's narrow drainage tailwater downstream from the dam. The lake was high. Water was exploding into the channel in a mesmerizing frothing. It was a sensory overload. The roar of the water. The cool mist on my face. His easy smile.

Without much conversation, we got back on the bike.

He put his hand on my knee and smiled, "You okay with some speed?"

"Oh, yes. How fast does this thing go?"

"I've had it up to a pack and a half," Mr. James Dean shouted over his shoulder as he moved the bike back onto the road. An empty straightaway. He smoothly opened the throttle, and the wind plastered my skin over my cheekbones. *Pack and a half,* I thought to myself, *that must be 150 mph.*

I barely survived the day. The first semi-sexual touch in oh, so long. Followed by a sultry departing hug and an open-ended invitation to some future dinner. I sizzled for days. My loins burned. I dreamed of hot sex. I waited eagerly to hear from him. The air sparkled with pheromones. This was way better than ballroom dancing lessons.

I didn't know what I wanted out of this; I was just following the scent. What was most obvious was the thickness of *what if* in the air. My brain running off on its own, thinking about what he might be like, what we might be like. It weaseled its way into every crack and crevice.

What if turned out to be nothing.

We made plans to go hunt for morel mushrooms. But whatever had been there on the bike by the dam evaporated in the woods. We couldn't get a conversation going. No traction. An awkwardness large between us. Still, when I didn't hear from him for days after, I called to make plans. Mr. James Dean said he didn't know, that he'd call back. He didn't, and I was relieved. I was glad to be rid of the *what ifs*. But surprised at my willingness to encourage the relationship even when I knew it wasn't right.

Over dinner one night just before a Bob Dylan concert, I outlined my dating dilemmas to an old girlfriend I had recently rediscovered.

"I don't even know what I'm looking for. A casual friend? Love? Someone to live with? And what about age? We're in the geezer health-decay zone. Heart attacks, Alzheimer's, cancer, arthritis. Would I end up nursing a man I hardly know? I'd rather not. I could hardly handle taking care of Jim."

She set a dish of steamed green beans on the table and looked at me with clear-blue intelligent eyes. "Remember being ten years old, how curious you were about everything, how free you were?" she asked. "Being past menopause is like being ten again. No bratty hormones in the way. We're free to be the clever girls we once were.

I don't date at all anymore. I've had all the lovers a girl could want. I've decided to leave sex at the curb for recycling and just be friends with men."

What an appealing idea! I could just skip sex altogether. I've had more sex than most – between my free-love hippie days and my many years as a single woman – why not just give it up? Have a massage if I needed to be touched. Enjoy the hugs from Emily and the many women who now populated my life. Touching doesn't have to be sexual.

Besides, it was easy to conjure up sexual memories – and so far they were more satisfying than the real thing. Even if I just focused on Jim. How many times had we had sex during all of our time together? Lots early on and less later, with breaks from time to time when things were rough. Say it averaged out to once a week. Over thirty years that would be more than fifteen hundred times. Even without sex as a priority, Jim and I had sex in every room of every house, in scores of motels and B&Bs, in tents, on beaches, mountain ridges and deserts, in boats, in garages, on couches, chairs, and car seats, in the bed of more than one pickup truck, in front of fireplaces, often in showers, annually in the woods. Wide-nostriled, hard-eyed sex. Dreamy, slow sex. Fast, ribald sex. Lazy morning sex. Incidental sex. Bored sex. Even when he was so sick, I used to slide naked into his bed in the mornings; we liked to start the difficult days skin to skin.

So as spring opened into this summer, I set about making new male friends. There was this tall, handsome guy I met at a conference. New in town, he approached me in a friendly but obviously sexy way. He was so old that he had served in Korea before I was in elementary school, but he was doing some interesting thinking on how religion makes people act irrationally.

"I'm not interested in romance," I said firmly to him. "But I would like to get to know you."

"Oh, no, I'm not either," he lied. "Friends. I'm good with that."

We got together on Sundays at his house in the suburbs. I helped him with his computer; we discussed writing, religion, work, and philosophy, had early old-folk dinners. He was a terrible cook. One day, after I pushed aside a partially eaten plate of burnt steak, gray broccoli, and a dry baked potato, he took my hand.

"I have to tell you. I always jack off after you go home. I can't help it. You are so sexy. Would you like to watch some porn? I have a great collection. It's just soft porn."

I pulled my hand back.

He leaned forward.

"Do you have a vibrator?"

"I thought you weren't interested in sex."

"I said I wasn't interested in romance. I don't want to fall in love. I don't want to get married again. I just want to have sex. Right now. I can give you the best orgasm you've ever had. Let me kiss you."

He got up from his chair and put his hand on my shoulder, turned my head with his other hand, and kissed me while I thought about how supremely bad I was at knowing what was really going on with guys. I pushed my chair back and stood.

"Really, I'm not interested in sex." And I wasn't. He wasn't appealing to me at all. I didn't need to smell his neck to know there was no chemistry for me with this guy. When I got home, a mean email from him was waiting for me. I deleted him from my contact list.

Being friends with men was harder than it seemed.

The next day by the paint section in Lowe's I ran into a man I hadn't seen since before Jim died. He had a smart but off-color wit; you could count on him for risqué Christmas cards and conversations punctuated with dirty jokes. He actually used to have the phrase *Widow Comforting* printed on his business card.

He'd read Jim's obit, gave his condolences, and then asked if I was dating.

I told him no.

The next day he called. Said he was a volunteer for a theater stage crew and sometimes had extra tickets for plays. Would I want to go? Said it wasn't a date. Just wanted someone to go with.

I said, "Ooh, okay."

In a couple more days he called to see if I'd go to a party with him. I reminded him that I wasn't dating.

He said, "It's not a date."

And then something kicked in: I got smarter for a nanosecond. I said No and No. No parties, no plays.

Then my soon-to-expire eHarmony account came up with a match to an earringed hunkerama. He was a classical-guitar-playing, photographer/graphic artist from a small town only five hours away who made me think I was still interested in sex. We pushed some promising emails slowly back and forth while I salivated over his photos. Even though he quit emailing me, I decided I wasn't done with sex.

Men persisted everywhere in my increasingly busy life. When not working until midnight or after on business projects, or getting the Prairie and the Point of Surrender installed, I went to plays, ate dinner, met for coffee, listened to music, watched movies, rode more motorcycles, and went on trips with men – mostly Dutch treat. I bought new underwear, lost weight, and started sleeping with guys just because they were so insistent.

Some were rich; some were not. Some were well-spoken; some stumbled over words. Some were sappy and wanted to fall in love in the worst way; some were black-hearted and wanted what they wanted. Every man I dated told me bitter stories of embattled childhoods, cruel fathers, and broken hearts. I got excited early and bored fast. I was a woman who rotated through men who rotated through women.

But so far I still didn't have a clue about what was going on. I would think we were having a good time, only to be asked what was wrong with me. I would think someone was upset, only to be scolded for making something of nothing. I lied to men and didn't tell them how I really felt, because I lied to myself.

In trying to sort out my confused feelings, I committed hours to examining the pros and cons of each guy. I made charts comparing no-go guys with new ones on key attributes: body types, lovemaking, conversation, home environment, emotional stability, friends, activities, computer skills, decrepitude, health, religion, how interesting they were, manner of argument, and approach to life.

Sex had been the centerpiece of all my relationships to date. I had tried to like sex as much as they did. I even had some very horny days. I used and didn't use condoms. I had a quickie in a state park shelter house and acquiesced to watch some porn. I discovered that these randy old goats, even with Viagra, have to pump and pump and pump and pump to get off – the opposite of young guys who discharge prematurely, neither of which made sex fun. I spent many sleepless nights in strange beds and many sleepless nights in my own bed with strange men. But the profile of overhanging bellies, the sheen of bald heads, and the farts in bed without the deepness of friendship left me flat and depressed.

Maybe it was this low-hanging-fruit collection of guys, but it seemed like every conversation was like that old email joke about how everything a guy says really means he wants to have sex:

I love you. = Let's have sex now.
I'm bored. = Do you want to have sex?
What's wrong? = I guess sex is out of the question right now.
Can I take you out to dinner? = I'd like to have sex with you.

The endless and affectionless sucking, licking, smooching, groaning, and buck buck bucking effectively deadheaded my fervor. And men knew it, because just as suddenly as my season of sex had begun, it ended. The swarm of men who had been teeming around me like house hornets went away.

*   *   *

After I got home from the market the next Saturday, I was sitting on my haunches by a freshly dug asparagus trench I was preparing for next spring when it sank in. I loved going to the market even though I didn't need any vegetables. I went for the people. I bumped into friends, caught up on the gossip, made quick plans for lunch or music later in the week. I talked about books, families, and trips. Projects, gardens, and dogs. It made me feel alive and whole.

My wild rush of men had been like horseweed pioneering a section of empty ground in the Prairie, but I wasn't as empty anymore. The part of me that had collapsed when Jim disappeared was beginning to fill in. I was putting down new taproots and holding my own.

I was the freest I had ever been. Jim's gift to me, the freedom to find another life, was bigger than just plugging in some other kind of guy. It was freedom from the concept of marriage that never fit me well anyway. Freedom to travel and think, to experiment again with life, to find new friends and have surprising conversations. Maybe I could rebuild that vacant side of me with the whole world.

What I had been doing over the summer, by not falling in love with these men, was starting to define who Jimless me was and wasn't, what was important and what was not. I'd been doing the same thing with women too. Trying out friendships – some sparking, some fizzling out. Letting selected old friends go, revitalizing others.

That didn't mean that I didn't still love necks. That I didn't like men. It didn't mean that I didn't still like Mr. Imaginary. It just meant that I had some more things to do before I sold the house, before I was a calm-assertive pack leader for the dogs, before I left the In Between.

15

Finding Boxerwood

The sign at the bank shimmered 99 degrees in the sweltering sun. Parked on a side street in tiny downtown Lexington, Virginia, I picked up my laptop from the passenger seat and shifted the glossy screen back and forth, dodging the persistent reflection of my sweaty face, bangs plastered and wilted like hydrangea leaves in the ruthless August sun. The poor dogs panted open-mouthed in the backseat. What I wanted was simple: to see the map to Boxerwood Garden. Was it too much to ask?

The cute hand-drawn map, hard to read in the daylight, was a digital file I had downloaded the night before at the B&B in Hot Springs. The dogs, who had to sleep in the car overnight, barked at every sound in the small parking lot. I'd gotten up early to steal away before the glares of fellow guests made for an uncomfortable breakfast.

Now here I was, stalled, trying to figure out how to get from this narrow street around the corner from Stonewall Jackson's house to Boxerwood Garden on the outskirts of town. Of course it would have been easier if I had remembered to print the map out before I'd left Indiana. Or if I had thought to write the directions down last night.

Sighing, I tried again, moving the laptop screen in infinitesimal increments until, like a Magic Eight Ball's *ask again later* answer, a legible map to the garden floated up through the glare. I unfolded the road map that was lying on the empty passenger seat and held it next to the screen to match up routes, trying not to move the computer one nano-inch. Randolph Street to Henry to Jefferson. Jog around White to Jackson. Take Ross to the left.

I was cranky on this road trip vacation, the first real one I'd had since Jim died, now a strangely distant but still near year and a half ago. Inconvenience clung to me. A little thing like ducking into an art gallery was a hopeless idea. There was no one to hold the dogs. They were too nervous to tie up outside on the street; Lila especially seemed to be channeling my grumpiness. And in this record heat there would be no lunch at the Red Hen restaurant on Washington Street. Leaving the dogs in the car, even in shade, was simply out of the question in this melting heat.

I should have taken Jim's old pickup with the nice ventilated, screened-in camper shell instead of my Honda Element with passenger windows that only wing open. I could hear his *I told you* so in my head. The bigger question was, why had I brought the dogs at all? Of course I had brought them – we had always taken the dogs on road trips. But I'd overlooked the fact that now there was no *we*, only me and the dogs. I had let the girls talk me into coming; they were sorry now, and so was I. I was especially sorry that Jim's opinions seemed to have wiggled his way into our vacation. This was supposed to be a getaway focused on me.

Virginia is thick with Arbogasts. An unusual name in Bloomington (a place settled by Buskirks and Rogerses), it's commonplace in these parts. When I'd registered at the B&B last night, the clerk had said, "That's a good valley name." Meaning Shenandoah Valley, of course. It made my heart swell a little to be recognized.

A few years ago Jim and I (and an earlier generation of dogs) had made it as far as Arbovale, West Virginia, on what I had thought was my roots vacation. Family lore had long held the town to be the original homestead; Daddy had said so. But recently my research had revealed that Daddy had been wrong. We came from the tiny town of Blue Grass, Virginia, twenty-four miles east over the mountain, not far from the bigger town of Monterey. That's where the original Arbogast immigrant had settled in 1766. Arbovale had been settled by a son, a brother of my direct ancestor. I wanted to go back, see the real place – now, while I was thinking about who I was. We were not taking a direct route, but a slow, two-week wander that had started in the bourbon and horse country of Kentucky, over the border, and up to the mountains of Highland County.

I had tried a vacation last year to southern New Mexico, thinking that the arid scrub desert would help me shake the buzz. That trip had been a bust. The room I booked at a B&B on the edge of town had smelled like mildew (in the desert – who would have guessed?). The husband who served the breakfast suffered from permanent brain damage due to an accident, making every morning too weird for me. Worse, the week I was there they closed further bookings and moved in the wife's mother, who was dying of cancer. A steady stream of hospice staffers came and went during the day, just in case I managed to forget Jim's dying for a moment or two.

There had been no getting away from the dreary circumstances that had followed me to New Mexico from Indiana, for the relatives that I was also visiting on this same trip were bitterly fighting as Alzheimer's raged through their days. In an early, hopeless effort to help me readjust to my job, my boss (the same one who later accused me of being griefless) had contacted the B&B and paid for my stay as a spa-retreat gift. She found my report of the trip unsatisfactory, as if I had purposefully found a way to flounder.

I had had higher hopes for this Virginia trip, but the scorching heat wave that was making news across the country for its record all-time highs was making it difficult. The dogs and I had been suffering in the 100-degree heat for days, but before heading up to the surely cooler mountains of Highland County, I wanted to see this garden.

According to its website, Boxerwood Garden was thirty-one acres divided into six distinct habitats with mature, naturalistically planted trees and shrubs. It was an enormous Point of Surrender planted over twenty years ago by a guy who had minimal interest in weeding, mowing, and mulching and a great interest in the endless variations of shrubs and in boxer dogs (he owned fourteen).

There were 2,500 cultivars and 4,500 native trees and shrubs, including 167 dwarf conifer varieties, 57 magnolia varieties, 81 dogwood varieties, 290 rhododendron and azalea varieties, and 154 Japanese maple varieties. The website also boasted of a self-guided tour. It didn't say anything about bringing dogs, but I figured with the boxer history it might work out.

Looking at the murky map on my laptop one more time, I committed it to memory, powered off the computer, and started driving down Randolph Street. Reciting the street names and turns as we went, I jig-jagged through neighborhoods peppered with swanky pillared and porched Georgian (or were they Federal?) houses peeking out behind lush gardens and wrought-iron fences. The neighborhood gave way to a winding, signless asphalt lane that I followed with faith.

Around a curve and past several low-lying brick ranch houses, Boxerwood's empty gravel parking lot suddenly appeared. I stopped under a scrawny pine tree that was parceling out scant shade. There was no one around. No clear welcome mats for, or warning signs against, dogs.

The girls were jumpy, skittish from the heat, but more because of my prickly attitude and the general pissiness I'd been sending their way as every step of my trip was made more difficult for having brought them, despite my having booked dog-friendly motel rooms for most of the trip. They knew things weren't good, but they weren't sure why, and they weren't having any fun. They hadn't been off the leash in days, the heat was unbearable, and they were worried about the constraints that came with each new day. They wanted me to turn around and go back home to Dog Paradise.

Jim used to say that dogs are a barometer of when it's time to leave. If they aren't having fun, you aren't either and it's time to go. But I wasn't leaving. I was on vacation, I was staying on vacation, and I was going to see this garden.

Lila glanced out the window with an anxious eye-roll and yawn. Diggity's tongue, spread wide, dripped saliva on the seat. Having been leashed, restrained, hushed, closed up, and increasingly miserable since we had left Indiana, they boiled out of the car when I opened the door, needing a good long run. Instead, I tied them to the undercarriage. I put out the battered and slightly hairy plastic bowl and filled it with Indiana water from the blue five-gallon container in the back of the car, explaining to the sorry eyes of the dogs, "I can't bring you until I find out if dogs can come. You stay in the shade. Try to relax."

I turned and walked maybe ten steps, kicking up a dry haze of uncertainty in the dust, before Lila let out a terrific howl. She had never been tied up before, and she certainly wasn't relaxed. Maybe she would settle down if I got out of sight. I quickened my pace to take the curve in the road that led from the parking lot. Her treble, accusing cries of abandonment pierced the thick air.

Surely any minute now a slightly chunky, wholesome woman bristling with multispecies sensitivity would pop up. Alarmed over Lila's cries, she would scold me about leaving, or bringing, or misunderstanding dogs. Instead, a dog bounded up. A boxer. She sprinted over to the girls. Balanced easily on her toes, stub of tail wagging, her friendly dog-nose checks ratcheted down the tension. Well, if there's one dog loose, there can be three. If Mrs. Do-Good showed up, I would just plead innocence.

The four of us walked down the dusty drive. The dogs charged around, knocking the edge off the claustrophobic humidity. As we approached a small weathered barn, an unfamiliar shape at its side caught my eye. I wasn't sure what it was. Not rusted saw blades, not wagon wheels, not a long-handled sickle scythe.

When I grew even with the barn, what I saw anchored me to the spot. It was three large rib bones artfully mounted on a red, rusty rectangle next to an enormous white, curving spine (a cow's?), all fixed on weathered wooden planks. The words SPARE RIBS were stenciled in white capital letters beneath.

Like a blast of cool air from a window air conditioner, this gust of nonsense permeated the humidity around me and opened a moment of freshness. A low, slow guffaw bubbled up in me.

The boxer and the girls bounced around me. "What's going on?" they nosed, sensing my nervous mood melting.

"Look," I snorted with a low har-har. "It's spare ribs." Lila dodged around my feet, and Digs stretched into a playful bow, rear end high in the air and white-tipped fluffy tail wagging. The boxer stood to the side, smiling and waiting.

I'm a fool for dumb jokes, like the Jumble word puzzle in the newspaper. Unscramble the letters to make four words. Arrange the circled letters to find the answer to a stupid joke suggested by the little cartoon:

> An unsharpened pencil is this [cartoon shows boy doing homework complaining to his mother about how his pencil doesn't work].
> Answer: *Pointless.*

I was unprepared for whimsy at Boxerwood. I expected propriety here among the rare shrubs, not goofiness on the side of a barn. The garden had a weighty mission to educate everyone "as to their place and role within a natural community." You'd think a garden with this heavy-duty mission would be solemn. How did this silly humor make it through the ever-narrowing filter of responsibility and the board of directors' approval?

The boxer loped off like Alice's rabbit down the hole, Lila and Digs in pursuit. "This way," they seemed to say, tongues lolling, tossing grins over their shoulders. "Down this path!"

The shaded trail meandered through rises of trees and shrubs and opened onto meadows. It curved into herb and vegetable alcoves and tucked into hidden nooks. Time relaxed. We discovered scattered ponds and stumbled onto exuberant vistas of the eastern Blue Ridge Mountains. Here, a kid-size tunnel made of live bent willows, a bedpost to support green beans, and a dangling tree canopy of wind toys. There, a painted, flying wooden owl and a mailbox next to a springhouse.

The girls played dart-around with the boxer and wallowed their bellies in soothing, stinky mud in a green pond.

Immense slabs of my grumpiness sloughed off like a hillside of heavy mud. I felt light, released of a tight weight I didn't know I carried. My shoulders unknotted. And my tender solar plexus, the now blackened place where I used to feel the shining gold cord that connected me to Jim, unclenched.

I strolled back to the Element in the parking lot, got a beer from the cooler, made a peanut butter sandwich, and headed for a bench under the dappled but deep shade behind the visitor center. On the way I noticed that the edges of the gardens and the paths were frizzy with forbidden grasses and weeds, plants that would normally be pulled, mulched, or poisoned away, especially in a display garden. Not only did whimsy rule here, but the messiness of life was allowed too.

This disordered goofiness of life and death was what was missing from every grief book I had read. In them, unlike in my world, all the deceased were canonized. All the survivors humble and broken. All the relationships perfect in retrospect. This isn't how life is, or death. Maybe I should abandon writing the mystery novel I was still slogging through and write a real story. The one that followed me around. Hopeless, absurd, bitter, transformational. Others out there needed to know they aren't alone in a flawed world. It was something to think more about when I wasn't so busy thinking about gardens.

Back home the Point of Surrender was beginning to show signs of trouble. Already in its young life, dandelions and knotweed were coming up in the beds and squirming their way into the creek-bed gravel trails that looped around the fruit trees. The wide-as-the-lawn-tractor grass pathway was widening as the creeping fescue blurred the tidy edges of the new beds.

But maybe that was okay. It was okay here at Boxerwood. Of course, this was an established garden, unlike my immature, weed-plagued effort at home.

Unlike gardens that are all about the subordination of nature to human reason and order, Boxerwood didn't take itself so seriously. It had its six distinct habitats, but there was an easy agreement that other unplanned plants could hang out here too. I hadn't seen any garden thugs like multiflora rose, Japanese honeysuckle, or stiltgrass, but I did sense a comfort level with garden evolution, decay, and renewal – and a clear understanding that stewardship did not equate to dictatorship.

When I was planning the Point of Surrender, I had in mind the famous Stowe garden in England. It is often pointed to as the prime example of landscape gardening. Once a proportioned formal garden, its symmetry was scrapped in the early 1700s when Viscount Cobham wanted a visual representation of the superiority of Whig free-market liberal thinking over the stiff ways of the Tory monarchy. In three phases over a forty-year span, three gardeners were charged with dismantling geometrical order and replacing it with irregular winding paths and the guise of wilderness vistas.

The last gardener was Lancelot "Capability" Brown. He had started young as a "gardener's boy" and ended up designing hundreds of big estate gardens. Capability earned his nickname through his effective marketing: part of his standard sales spiel was to tell people their estates had a "great capability for landscape improvement." Like a wooing garden catalog. He converted Stowe to a park of undulating grasses, woodlands, clumps, and beltways. He thought of his work as punctuating the landscape. He would refer to a flower bed as a comma or a semicolon. He set areas off in parentheses. He started new subjects after planting a period. His garden, though, like freedom, was not linear. There was no central point from which to view the garden; one had to walk through it to experience it – just like life. That's what had caught my attention when I was planning the Point of Surrender.

The Stowe garden was an imperfect model for me. It was just as artificial as a formal garden. Capability's sweeping landscapes were carefully composed and managed by scores of gardeners. It was more about replicating landscape paintings than the reality of how plants, trees, and grasses liked to grow.

All gardeners are like Capability; they want to establish a clear character in their gardens. Every garden is a demonstration of some moral, political, artistic, or philosophical value. Widely spaced plants as single specimens or mingled, vegetables in rows or staggered, trimmed hedges or unpruned shrubs, raised beds or containers, edged beds or overlapping ground covers – each delivers a different message.

But choices in my present life were limited. I had a house I couldn't sell with a two-acre garden and no gardening staff or volunteers to help, not enough money for routine garden help. I might want tidy edges, I might want a tiny civilized garden in town, but that wasn't what I had. My real world, like my garden, was jumbled and intermixed. Since there was no making it otherwise, I needed to just lighten up about the whole thing, keep this light, sloughed-off feeling, and embrace my frizzy garden as a true representation of my life.

16

Crabbottom Grits

I took the curve slowly around the tip of Jack Mountain and down through steep stands of oak, hickory, and red spruce forest. We had just finished taking a break on the border of Highland County for some leashless romping in the cool mountain laurel thickets. The dogs, happy, paws pungent from leaf litter, smiled in the rearview mirror.

Most people know this road as Route 250, but a zoom-in on Google had showed that it is also Hanky Mountain Highway, or Shenandoah Mountain Road. I wanted these names, instead of 250, next to the bright yellow triangle warning signs with pictograms of semi-trucks pointing at dangerous downhill angles over the words NEXT 2 MILES. Some sense of place instead of clear direction.

From the Virginia map calculations I had made at the B&B the night before, I knew there were three mountains between Monterey and the big Shenandoah Valley. First Shenandoah, then Bull Pasture, and now Jack. At the center of this Appalachian geologic uplift, where some 480 million years ago the earth folded and buckled like pie crust, Highland County calls itself Little Switzerland, although it is really defined not by the elongated mountains and scattered knobs, but by the tabletop valleys in between. You won't see such valleys in the young, spiky Rocky Mountains; this is the stuff of old mountains.

There are five fertile valleys in Highland County. Their straight-forward names had made me smile: Alleghany, Bluegrass, Monterey, Bullpasture, and Cowpasture. This is where the towns, villages, and hamlets were. This is where the sheep and cows grazed. This is where my ancestor Michael Arbogast settled.

The windows were down, the air was soft. As the curve opened up, Monterey gently revealed itself in the valley below. I pulled onto the shoulder of the road on the rise to admire how the town was tucked neatly into the hollow. It looked like a picture that would be used for a jigsaw puzzle. The white church and steeple with red tin roof. Main Street bisecting a scattered grid of buildings. The hazy mountains beyond.

Unseen beyond the next ridge were the parallel roads, High Road and Low Road, that crossed Blue Grass Valley to converge at the town of Blue Grass, the original home of the Arbogasts. My ancestors surely had walked on the streets of Monterey. It was the county seat. Maybe they came in for land titles or for livestock auctions, maybe to listen to some fiddle music at a maple syrup season dance, certainly to muster for the Revolutionary and Civil Wars.

We descended into town, the temperature rising as we came down the mountain road. I drove slowly, gawking, finally stopping and parking in front of the Highland Inn, which rambles down a third of a block in the middle of town. Even though I had a cabin reserved in the mountains outside of town, the inn's broad steps beckoned me. I told the girls I wouldn't be long as I left them for a quick look inside.

I ran my fingers along the smooth wood railing next to drowsy sunflowers as I walked up the steps and paused in the shade of the inn's two-story, white-spindled porch that ran across the front of the building. A line of rocking chairs shifted slightly in the hot breeze. Old school benches flanked the door.

I pushed open one side of the inn's green double doors. A floral patterned rug ran up a stout staircase leading to rooms upstairs. To the left was a front desk window framed in thick, dark wood of decorative moldings, casings, and corner blocks. A silver service bell sat on the counter, but no clerk was there. Craning my neck around the corner, I peeked into the room down the hall. It was a library for slow travelers, packed with murder mystery novels. Monopoly, Clue, and Candy Land games stacked high. Behind me, the clatter of dishes and the murmur of low conversations drifted from a dining room. White cloths, a lazy ceiling fan, shades pulled down halfway. Posted on a doorway leading to the back was a menu for the Black Sheep Tavern that would be open later. *Highland's Own Rainbow Trout. Maple Pecan Pie.*

I wanted to ring the desk bell, chat with the clerk, have my bags taken up the substantial stairs. I wanted to sit in the shaded rockers on the porch with a book lazily open in my lap, listen to stories of other travelers, maybe join someone for dinner and linger, laughing, over the trout. But I wasn't staying here, even though they accepted dogs. I had promised the girls that we would chill out in the mountains.

A wall of heat hit me as I returned to the broad porch. I wanted to explore a bit, walk down Main Street. I opened the door to the Element and leashed the dogs as they looked around nervously at an unknown they preferred to avoid. They had hoped we were done with hot.

We were alone on the sun-bleached sidewalk; sensible people were in the shade, in front of fans, or secluded in air conditioning. A line of clapboard storefronts and a couple of log buildings sat tight against the sidewalk. As I peered through windows, I saw no one. On an iron bench by a white picket fence sat a person made of clay pots, with flowering plants for hair and hands. It all seemed a bit too bucolic and quirky for Arbogast territory, and I wondered if Boxerwood's spirit of whimsy had somehow floated on the air over the mountains and infected this town.

Across the street a deep lawn opened to a brick courthouse. Its white façade – four elephantine pillars capped by a classic triangular gable with a half-sunburst-paned window – was like a temple to the antebellum days. Instead of a fountain there stood a statue of a farm-boy soldier still watching for troops from the north. On the corner, in the window of the H&H Cash Store, next to a poster for maple syrup and buckwheat flour was a sign: *If we don't have it, you don't need it.*

That's more our style. The Arbogasts, and Virginians in general, have a history of being cantankerous, with no-nonsense ways. Self-reliant and full of tightly held sentiments. Family tales abound of spats and grudges; cousins, siblings, and parents never speaking again to cousins, siblings, and children. I didn't get to be as opinionated as I am by accident.

Supposedly the men of the first American Arbogast family were formidable – more than two-hundred pounds, over six feet tall, and long-lived, some to more than a hundred years. Captain Jacob Seybert, when commenting on the Shawnee massacre of 1758 in neighboring Augusta County, reportedly said, if the Arbogasts had been there he could have held the place in spite of the Indians.

There's rarely a mention of the Arbogast women, but I'm guessing they were just as good at surviving and looking out for their own interests. As a clan, we're excellent at pulling ourselves up by our bootstraps and getting on with things. We've got a lot of grit, if a little dry in the humor department.

Here in Monterey a balance had been struck. Boxerwood whimsy and Arbogast contrariness coexisted.

The heat of the midday sun forced the girls and me back into the Element and the rush of the air conditioning. Accelerating out of town, I passed the Arbogast Inn at the end of Main Street, a white Victorian B&B with a tin roof. The thrill of being in Arbogast country grew as I wound my way through the fourteen miles of mountain road toward our cabin retreat and cooler air.

In order to rent the cabin I had been forced to agree to keep my dogs restrained so that they would not attract bears, kill sheep, or cause trouble. They didn't know this, of course, so as we turned off the highway onto a gravelly road through dense woods, up the steep hill to the long ridge drive of Bear Mountain that bisected the high pastures with West Virginia sprawled out on one side and Virginia on the other, they thought of nothing but running free. They were sure of it when an unleashed, big, fluffy yellow dog greeted us when we pulled up.

But, no, they were not to be free, and neither was I, until I quit resisting. Rules dictated I had to keep the dogs tied when they were outside the little rustic cabin I had rented. I had hoped to tether them to the shady porch so that I could go into town without them, but Lila would have none of it, screeching every time I tried.

We were tethered together but not crowded. Our humanless existence that had started at Boxerwood and persisted in Monterey, made itself at home with us. We were the only occupants in a little cluster of cabins. No Internet connection, no cell phone.

Mornings we took long walks through woods and fields that fluttered orange with monarchs on milkweed. Little painted bear paw signs marked the trails as if the Boxerwood spirit had found its way here too. A shaded rocky overhang, thick with moss next to an old maple to lean against, made for comfortable afternoon reading.

Evenings collapsed into a lazy meal and the stack of novels, dogs napping at my feet. At dusk the landowner played the flute on her porch around a hill from my cabin. Ethereal music as the sun disappeared behind the mountains. I thought about how to take Boxerwood home with me. Maybe make a willow-way tunnel, add little jokes like the Spare Ribs sign here and there. I drew up some plans in my journal.

One afternoon I flipped open my laptop to work on my murder mystery but instead started an essay about Boxerwood. The Spare Ribs, the boxer, freedom, frizzy grass, the need for some lightness in my life, how gardens and life reflect each other. About the raw truth of grieving, about difficult love. I thought I might be at the beginning of something interesting, maybe a book called "The Garden Chronicles."

Some nights I slipped into the hot tub a few steps away from my cabin. Glass of wine, the Milky Way rotating enormous overhead. I stayed up late marathoning the ten Woody Allen DVDs that I'd brought with me, the laptop glowing blue in the dark of the cabin. Yes, the improbable farce of it all.

On Friday, as our week was coming to an end, I roused my restored self and loaded up the girls to go find the town of Blue Grass and explore the Arbogasts.

Blue Grass hadn't always been called Blue Grass. When my forbearers lived here it was first called Hull's Store – Arbogast land abutted Hull land, and one of the Arbogast sons married a Hull daughter. Later the town's name changed to Crabapple Bottom, then shortened to Crabbottom, which caused many embarrassing jokes for men sent out to the broader world in World War II. When they came home, the soldiers petitioned to get the name changed to Blue Grass in 1950.

I drove back east over the mountains down into the scalding valley. Turning at Hightown, I poked down Low Road through Blue Grass Valley, past Wistful Vista Road, into the few blocks of Blue Grass. There was a hot, hilly cemetery on the edge of town. I didn't recognize any of the Arbogast names there. I stopped in the general store, feeling the eyes of every resident on my out-of-town orange Element. The screen door slapped with tradition behind me as I walked in. At the counter the slightly doughy clerk glared at me, knowing my shopping list would be short and guessing I could be a bother. I looked for something, anything I could buy to commemorate the moment and start a conversation.

Grabbing a bottle of expensive local maple syrup and a can of Mountain Dew soda, I cozied up to the counter and put on my best friendly smile. "Sure is a hot day."

"Yep," said the clerk, looking at me with flat eyes.

"I was wondering," I said as I handed her cash, "do you know where the original Michael Arbogast house might be?"

She shrugged. "Nope," she said sharply to cut off the conversation before it could begin.

I needed some advice, but I wasn't going to get it here.

On the way back to the car, I remembered a sign in Monterey about a Friday afternoon market. Maybe someone there would know. I took out my map and memorized a route around Ginseng Mountain, turning at Forks of Water, and following Strait Creek Valley into town.

Sure enough, on Main Street there stood a silly scarecrow dressed in a flannel shirt, jeans, work gloves, and a floppy hat leaning against the Spruce and Main Street post. From his right arm hung a sign: FARMERS MARKET was stenciled in uneven red capital letters. FRIDAY 3:30–6 was painted underneath and scrunched to one side in the custom of all hand-lettered signs. An arrow pointed the way. I was in luck; this was Friday.

Down Spruce Street, next to an old school turned community center, I found the market. A small rectangle of tables in a picnic shelter offered a scattering of measly, thin-mountain-air tomatoes and peppers between plastic bags of homemade zucchini bread, blueberry muffins, and noodles. A far cry from the almost obscene, fat bounty of Indiana's August harvest. At one table, next to jars of blueberry jam, sat a pile of spiral-bound, laminated books – *The Arbogast Family Cookbook*.

I flipped one open. Just before the table of contents and a few hundred nostalgic recipes using canned vegetables for pot pies and instant rice for casseroles, there was a family portrait that had been taken in front of a big house. The names underneath were not familiar.

As I handed over twelve dollars for the book, I searched the man behind the table for recognizable features, but saw none. "Are you an Arbogast?" I asked.

"Grandson to Carl and Marie," he said, pointing to the picture.

"Would you sign under the photo for me? I'm an Arbogast. From Indiana."

A slow smile perked up his face as he reached for a pen.

"Do you know where the original Arbogast house is?" I asked.

He handed me back the book and said, "Yes, that's a picture of it. We live there."

Then the woman standing next to me said, "We live in one too. They're everywhere. Who is your Arbogast relative?"

I rattled off the male side of my father's lineage. They told me my cousin, who volunteered over at the Highland Museum in McDowell, ten miles to the east, would probably know that house. They wrote down the phone number. I turned on my cell phone and made an appointment.

The next morning, as the girls and I drove the thirty-five miles from the cabin to the museum, a trip that would have taken Michael two or three days, I summoned up all I had been able to learn about these Arbogasts, sorry that no stories about my ancestors had been passed down. That no one cared enough to remember.

Michael Arbogast had landed at the Port of Philadelphia along with about thirty thousand other Germans who arrived during a massive six-year exodus. They were recruited by the Brits to settle the region as a buffer against Indian attacks, Catholicism, and French expansion. Germans and Irish were recruited because skilled workers, needed for the booming textile and iron factories of the British early industrial revolution, were not allowed to emigrate. Neither were the Germans, but it didn't stop them.

It was hard times in southwestern Germany in 1749. People were short on food, highly taxed, and persecuted if they weren't Catholic – and eager to leave once they heard how wonderful America was. Virginia was pitched by salesmen, called Newlanders or Soul Traders, who were sent to Germany to recruit the settlers. Like timeshare sales con artists, they picked up a commission for each contract (written in English) they got signed.

These salesmen were immigrants themselves who had been hired to go back to the homeland and persuade fellow countrymen to leave. Dressed in beautiful clothes to demonstrate their recently acquired wealth, they gave garden-catalog-worthy descriptions of the land. An early Lutheran minister wrote that the Soul Traders gave "descriptions of America as make one believe it to contain nothing but the Elysian fields, bearing seed of themselves, without toil and labor, mountains full of solid gold and silver, and wells pouring forth nothing but milk and honey, etc. Who goes as a servant, becomes a lord; who goes as a maid, becomes a milady; a peasant becomes a nobleman; a citizen and artisan, a baron!"

It took about four months and lots of cash, or debt, for the emigrants (who had to sneak out of Germany, since it was illegal to leave) to get to the port at Rotterdam and onto a ship. Then, packed in like herrings, another couple months to cross the ocean. Once in port, they couldn't get off the ship until they swore allegiance to the Crown and could pay their passage or negotiate a slave-work contract for several years. Then they would be free.

Michael was just seventeen years old when he boarded the ship *Speedwell,* probably a large two-masted brig with square sails, along with 240 other emigrants. His mother, father, and sisters were all dead. He was the only son.

Ten years later he was living in Virginia, naturalized, married to a second-generation Virginia woman, and, I bet, speaking English fairly well. Not only did he buy the line of the Soul Trader's spiel, but he also lived it. By his mid-thirties he had started accumulating property and was well on his way to becoming one of the largest landowners around, more than a thousand acres. There were seven admired sons and two unremarked-upon daughters. Michael and his three eldest sons (including my great-great-great-great-grandfather David) fought in the Revolutionary War and survived. One son fought in and survived the War of 1812.

*   *   *

The blanched dry fields sped by, fields Michael would have known. White picket fences announced McDowell, which was really just a few houses along the road. It was easy to find the old house – it was the only brick house in town. It was a Hull family house built in the 1800s that had served as a Stonewall Jackson headquarters, a Civil War hospital, a hotel, a stagecoach stop, and now a museum.

I left the girls in the Element under a lone tree several blocks away, every possible window open, water dish filled to the brim, and calculated I had an hour before the sun moved from behind the tree to beat down on them. A stray breeze moved through the thick air. Maybe it was slightly less hot here.

My elderly cousin was waiting for me upstairs at a heavy wooden table in a room lined with genealogy books. The slight scent of mildew tickled my nose. An air conditioner cranked noisily in the window.

My shorts and T-shirt seemed disrespectful next to his white pressed shirt and brown suit and tie. He listened to me recite my lineage, nodding his head at each generation. Elizabeth and Michael. Elisabeth and David. Katherine and Enos. Isabele and Sanford. Cordelia and Enos. Pearl and Straud. Maxine and Elmore.

"Yes, I know your family," he said. "And I know where the old house is."

I unfolded a map and scooted it across to him. He ran his thin, smooth fingers over the web of back roads.

"The old house is here," he said, tapping at the map with his index finger. "In the field behind a newer house. As you drive around this curve you can just see it. It's before the road turns to gravel and goes up the mountain. It was in Arbogast hands until a few years ago, but they had to sell."

Three hours later I pulled the car over onto a small grassy shoulder in the curve of road next to a flock of sheep, the dogs whining to chase the herd. I thought this spot might be where my cousin had pointed to on the map. There was an old house set back far away. I couldn't really see. The air undulated in the broiling sun.

And then it hit me. It didn't matter if this was the house or not. What mattered was how Michael had broken free from the restraints and traditions of the old ways to find a new way in a new land. He had left the old wars and taken on new ones. While others cried and whined over being duped by the Soul Traders, he served his time and made his dream happen.

Who knows what misery and horror he might have seen, being the only survivor of his German family, who may have been wasted by typhoid fever or mowed down in war. But Michael built a better life on the disaster of their deaths. As surely as he mourned them, he lived proudly and made Arbogast a name that rings with honor across the Shenandoah Valley.

My Jim and career disasters seemed so shallow in comparison and my bleak grief over the loss of the former me so indulgent. But one thing was for sure: my life was getting better. I wasn't headed for just a different life, but a better one and a better me. One that would not be here if Jim were alive. And it was time to be grateful and unabashed about living it.

This is verboten thinking. Widows and left-behind lovers are never supposed to say this. We're supposed to say that our relationships and marriages were perfect. *You were crazy in love. It's like half of you is gone. He was everything to me.* Once your main squeeze kicks the bucket, the union, no matter how complicated or imperfect, becomes sacrosanct. The dead one golden and wonderful, the one left behind without a reason to go on. All the bad times must fall away, and only the good times can remain.

We are allowed to stumble onward, bravely. We are allowed to heal and learn to enjoy life again. We are allowed to love again. But we are not supposed admit that life is better after a lover's death.

I needed to write about this, but I didn't want to. People would think it was cathartic, therapy writing, a cleansing. A way for me to process my emotions. But I was doing just fine processing. I didn't even think I was forging new ground. All I was doing was walking a path walked by many but unspoken of, and these important things needed to be said out loud.

It's not that I was glad that Jim was dead, but he was. And because of the chaos of his death I had a chance to break out of my crystallized and hardened patterns of predictability, to crack the calcified static of my life. In the rubble of Jim's illness and death, I had a chance to walk into the next stage of my life with a new perspective. Some people never have, or take, this chance; instead they become frozen into who they are, what they think, how they act.

Now I didn't have to take the dogs on vacation with me anymore.

17

Peripheral Vision

The next time I found myself sweltering hot for days at a time it was January, and I was dogless, in a place that couldn't be more different from Virginia, or from Indiana for that matter.

I was alone and slowly limping down a side street near Khao San Road, the gritty, crowded, budget-backpacker ghetto of Bangkok, with fifteen crippling blisters on my feet. Every inch of my body was dripping in sweat even though the cruel midday sun had long passed. There are two temperatures in Bangkok: hot and hotter. I was there during hot, and I couldn't imagine how hot hotter was.

Over my head was a beautiful paper parasol, more Japanese-looking than Thai, painted with white dancing cranes, bonsai-like pines, and round red suns. I'd bought it from a street vendor outside the high walls of the bedazzling Grand Palace and Temple of the Emerald Buddha. But the stench of uncured varnish on the paper umbrella, heated in the unrelenting sun and mixed with the thick, ochre pollution in the air, was anything but beautiful and it had teased up a slight headache. My lower gut was threatening to explode, again, and I nervously wondered if I might have to find another filthy pit toilet, hopefully without a line of tourists.

The day had been full of arguing with cheating taxi drivers and wandering in the boiling heat (wearing a long, palace-provided sarong to cover my inappropriate legs) through acres of gleaming gold-encrusted monuments, spires, pagodas, Buddhas, dragon devils, and monkey gods amid ornate tile-and-mirror mosaics and ancient painted murals. I had managed to successfully alienate my gracious traveling companions, who had invited me to join them on this trip by complaining about staying in hostels for twenty-somethings, wanting more say about our itinerary, and generally being wimpy about eating local food. Nothing like a vacation to test a friendship.

I had begged off my friends and gotten away from all the tourists onto a side street, carefully noting my turns so that I could find my way back to the chaos of the food vendors and the crush of people. There was not a single sign in English and not a familiar tongue being spoken. And I was outrageously happy, loving every minute of my crazy, exotic, difficult, unexpected vacation when a brick wall of sadness hit me. A walloping undefined melancholy. It stayed with me all the way south to the Ko Phi Phi Islands in the Indian Ocean and traveled back with me to the busy subways and scooter-packed streets of a wet, cold Taipei and then home to frozen Indiana.

A fundamental sadness. Frequent, deep, sob-wracked weeping. It stayed with me for two months. I awoke with it and walked with it and ate with it and slept with it. This was a different kind of crying than the numb, buzzy tears that fell from my eyes shortly after Jim's death. It was so annoying. I am not a woman who often cries.

As February came up, the important anniversary dates on my calendar jerked me hard, much harder than the year before. The sixth anniversary of buying the house together. The second anniversary of Jim's death. The looming It Means Absolutely Nothing wedding anniversary in March followed immediately by Jim's birthday. I had written them down because I kept forgetting them, and I wasn't allowed to forget those dates. I didn't understand it until I took my sadness to Mexico.

Since Virginia I'd been dishing out dollars by the bucket-load on travel. My business was thriving, I had the money to go on trips, and I was able to work my independent schedule around them. I had spent the New Year holiday in Mexico, left a few weeks later for Thailand,

and then returned to Mexico in March to a timeshare I had purchased on my first visit.

The timeshare, Hacienda del Mar, was on the tip of Baja. Twenty-eight acres with hacienda-style villas, fountains, a white sand beach, five restaurants, and flawless gardens. I had attended a sales presentation in order to get a big discount on a car rental. I'd brought all the cynicism I could muster to the appointment, certain I would never buy. And I went home with an interest-free payment plan and an annual vacation in a dogless paradise for the next twenty years. As part of the signing bonus, I'd gotten a free week in March, when it was hot, but not too hot.

Even though I was still schlepping my melancholy around, I was not immune to the wind rustling the palm fronds off my balcony or the perfect azure blue of the Sea of Cortez beyond red clay tile roofs. I leaned on the iron railing and looked down to a tangerine-colored hibiscus blooming below.

Left to its own devices, this Mexican garden would be a dry, scrub desert like the land that surrounded it. But it was not, thanks to the scores of gardeners watering, weeding, and nodding hello. Unlike my gardens, here every detail was tended. This was a garden of clear intentions. The curve, the pacing, the shape, the variation, the color, the nuance, the exuberance, and the filtering of light all had been thought out carefully.

I gathered my floppy orange sun hat and stuffed my book into my beach bag, thinking the only decision I would have to make that day was what to have for dinner, and left my small villa to follow a flagstone walkway between squared-off bougainvillea hedges of fuchsia, peach, white, deep red, and pale pink past the occasional mosaic tile fountains. My sadness heeled next to me like a good dog.

Couples eddied around me, holding hands, as I slowly made my way toward the beach. Mostly older, with spiny legs and poochy bellies. They had a smoothness about them, and I imagined them to have weathered changes together, to be good friends, or at least not overly restless about their relationship.

I wondered why there weren't more uncoupled travelers here, other solo adventurers. I often chatted up other women by the pool, in the shuttle, in lobbies. I'd start off asking, "Oh, do you know a good restaurant in town for fresh fish?" or sweetly complimenting them, "What a pretty dress."

These were usually brief exchanges. The women edged away from me, distancing themselves from my singleness or perhaps uncomfortable with a stranger being so forward. I was learning how to talk to strangers and made small talk wherever I went. It didn't always go the way I thought it would.

Yesterday, on my excursion to the marina in town, I had struck up a conversation with the waiter at the dockside restaurant. After a bit, he said he could be my Mexican boyfriend. "I'm available for the evening," he said in perfect English. This was not the conversation I had hoped for.

"Where is your husband?" This is a question I was asked over and over again in marriage-oriented Mexico. I had started saying, "Dead, *muerto*," to cut off inquiries, but wondered what I would have said if Jim and I had never married, or what divorced women said, or what I might have said instead to get across the understanding that being bundled up with someone is not a requirement for happiness.

I emerged from the garden walkway to a series of connected swimming pools that perched between the villas and the beach. As I walked by the poolside chairs, an older woman stopped me.

"Are you here alone?" she asked.

She looked familiar. I'd seen her on other days carefully walking and had thought to myself: *That's me in a few years.*

"Yes," I said. I set my bag of books, notebooks, and water down and knelt beside her, noticing how her delicate breasts lightly filled a lacy bra-like swim top.

"I thought so," she said. "You are always by yourself."

"I love it here," I said, changing the subject and gesturing to the landscape. "I love the gardens."

"Me too," she said. "I had big gardens for years but had to sell my house and move to a condo. I miss them so much. I had colon cancer, chemo." She rushed on. "You look like you tan evenly. I blotch."

Our conversation could have bloomed; we could have been friends. I could have talked to her about how I wished I could trade my house and gardens for a little place in town, but instead I stumbled over words about getting sun poisoning in the tropics and staying in the shade and wearing my wide-brimmed hat.

"I'm not here to get a tan," I said, gathering my things.

I was edging away from her just like other women did me. Was it the cancer and chemo that I couldn't bear to be around? Was it the category of the vulnerable old woman I resisted? In the mirror last night I noticed that the old-age spot on my left cheek had become fairly prominent. The other day I had caught my reflection in the glass door of the spa: a me with old-lady legs. Old was coming without asking.

"I'm here for a tan," she said. "I'm from Connecticut. If you are ever that way, you could visit. Our winter has been terrible. Snow up to here," she said raising her pale, thin arm. "Maybe we can have dinner. I'm here for two weeks."

I wrote down her room number and told her mine. "Sure, I'll call you," I lied, knowing that I wouldn't.

As I settled into my beach chair under my very own wide, green patio umbrella stuck in the sand with an icy beer on a side table (all brought to me by a smiling attendant who always seemed to know when to appear and when to disappear), it occurred to me that Jim would hate this Mexican resort. He would think it was too, too put together. He would translate the attendant's measured hospitality as unctuousness. He would be mean and surly, would drink too much.

All the things he wouldn't like, I did. This was a weed-free escape from my scruffy, dogged life. Here I had nothing to do. People scrambled to make me comfortable. Everywhere I looked, life was perfect. I didn't care if it was an artificial, staged fantasy. It was what I needed.

It was then that I realized why I had been crying. It was because I was leaving Jim, and really this time. I was leaving the Jimless me for the new me. I was making memories that didn't have him in them. Going places he couldn't come, wouldn't want to be. There would be no going back, no reconciliation. My new better life was a casting out of him, a turning away from the things that used to be.

I stretched out in the cushioned lounge chair and let my funky melancholy go. The waves crashed up onto the sand and retreated, taking my heaviness with them. The changing surface of the sea caught my attention – restless, surging, relentless, corrugated, puckered, stippled, shirred, transient, frothy, lacy. The ocean was comfortable being all of those things, and I could be comfortable being more than one way too. I lifted my eyes to the horizon, where the edge of the indigo water met a pale sapphire sky. Its wide foreverness filled both sides of my peripheral vision. Before me I imagined I could see the slight curve of the earth.

That night I had dinner under the elegant open-air thatched palm roof of the resort's five-star restaurant that overlooks the ocean. It was a swanky Pacific Rim Asian fusion splurge for me. Wicker rattan chairs, spotlights on the palms. A smooth samba trio. Coconut curry creamed asparagus soup with lobster chunks. Blackened swordfish with mango papaya relish.

As I watched the sun turn the sky violet and apricot, I opened my journal to the Seven Stages of Grief I had written down the previous year. My grief had never matched up quite right.

Sipping on a scotch, its smoky flavor mingling with bites of decadent chocolate cake and ginger ice cream, I made adjustments:

The Seven Stages of Grief, Revised

1. Not shock and denial, but giving in to the buzz
2. Not disorganization, but being stronger than plugged drains
3. Not violent emotions, but hippie-chick dancing
4. Not guilt, but lingering in the In Between
5. Not loss and loneliness, but getting rid of the lawn
6. Not relief, but facing the truth
7. Not reestablishment, but leaving the dogs at home

When I returned home from my week in paradise, I would crawl under the potting table in the green garden shed, pull out the seed trays, and get everything going under the grow lights. It was just six weeks until the first of May. Maybe the house would sell this year, maybe it wouldn't.

On the table in the dining room eleven seed packets sat in a finely turned oak bowl that I had bought on my Virginia roots vacation: Purple Podded Pole Beans, Clairmore Zucchini, Orient Express Cucumber, Detroit Red Beet, Mt. Fuji Morning Glory, Cappuccino Rudbeckia, Van Gogh Sunflower Mix, Crazy Daisy Shasta Daisy, Panorama Monarda, Mallow Myst Hollyhock, and Only the Lonely Nicotiana. Seeds carefully chosen from wickedly beautiful garden catalogs. I knew that some would take root and thrive in my frizzy gardens, and some would not.

18

Six Years Later: New Tricks

It's a gorgeous garden under these weeds, packed under this layer of dense grass sod. I can feel it in the rich, black loam. Neglected for a decade or so, this plot, once a productive organic vegetable garden, is hungry.

It wants to grow tomatoes taller than me, bending with the heavy weight of heirloom crimson-fleshed globes. It wants Italian zucchini to cast giant palms of leaves over the ground to hide squash so that they can become the size of footballs. It wants rows of rainbow chard with stalks of hot pink, electric yellow, and flame orange next to crisp cucumbers with tendrils reaching for the sky. Dangling green beans that must be picked every day.

It wants bone, blood, shit, and ashes. Nitrogen, phosphorous, digested organic matter, and calcium potassium in less personal terms.

Crumbly dirt sifts through my fingers as I break up clods, toss stones out into the alley. I drag myself up from the duckwalk squat I've held for too long and shove the spade into the ground. It goes in deep before dead-walling into the clay. I can feel the spirit of the gardener who worked this land before me. His dogged persistence, his arrogant righteousness, his abstract passion, his wry humor.

I walk over to sit on the limestone step at the back of the house. Sweat stings my eyes. I wipe my drippy nose on the hem of my T-shirt. An innocent April breeze cools my face. The water in my BPA-free metal bottle is sweet, like the water of my childhood, the water in that galvanized bucket in my grandmother's garden.

Before me stretches a long rectangle of green. To its side runs a gravel alley with a strip of grass down the middle. Nearest me, a square of revealed black dirt. I figure a week, maybe a bit more, to weed and slowly roll back the sod if it doesn't rain. Then the tilling in of the bone, blood, shit, and ash. And a weed barrier of newspaper covered with squares of straw sheaves to keep the moisture in when the August drought comes. Too bad I didn't know I was going to work this garden last year; then I would already have had bales of nice rotted straw.

This reclaiming is a major project of note. One worth recording. I pull the iPhone out of my back pocket, snap a photo, and upload it to my "Veggie Garden" album on Facebook with the comment: *And so it begins.* Then I walk the block and a half home.

My new house sits high away from any seeping springs or pooling patios, but close to the sidewalk. Jim has never been here and his stuff isn't here either – I auctioned off almost everything, including the pickup truck, when I bought this tiny home after finally selling Elwren four years ago.

Its gardens, once unruly and ill-conceived, are now well-behaved and lush. My favorites replicated – thyme, oregano, Asian lilies, pink echinacea with orange cones, columbines, hostas, and ferns – in stone-walled beds. No evil fescue pasture grass is trying to bully its way in here.

Two trusty Limelight hydrangeas flank the front steps. There are peonies, of course – double pink Sarah Bernhardt; red, lusty Karl Rosenfield; delicate, white Crinkled Linens.

And there are new ideas like the French Lace weigela bush with ruby-red flowers and variegated leaves that struts its stuff every June by the end of the driveway. Last year this garden won an award from Bloomington in Bloom, as one of the Best Spring Yards.

The Point of Surrender it's not. There's no Dog Paradise. And no Tick Acres or doomed Prairie. Only half an acre. A postage stamp lot.

But I count all of my neighbor's gardens as mine. All the twenty-five acres of three neighborhoods: Prospect Hill, Near Westside, and Maple Heights. Planted and tended by others. Blocks graced with fleshy pink magnolias. Scores of arching, fragrant lilac bushes. Thousands of perky daffodils. Gazillions of peonies nod in Rose Hill Cemetery, where Bob Dylan once put a penny on Hoagy Carmichael's grave.

Cars whiz by just a half block away, yet when I sit on the white front porch swing of my sweet, green bungalow, all I hear is the *pretty, pretty, pretty* song of cardinals, a busy city flock that bustles in the thick silver maples that shield my house from the hot southern sun. It's the dream I had for so long: a little house with a little garden in town. And it's even a new house, built to look old, with modern plumbing, insulation, and open rooms.

It's a wonderful place to write – upstairs, downstairs, on the deck, on the porch, at the kitchen counter – and I have so many writing projects going I can't keep up. "The Garden Chronicles" quit being essays and arranged itself into a book that's been written, rewritten, revised, reorganized, reworked, reread, and renamed *Leave the Dogs at Home.*

The elderly girls are now spry city dogs who call a deck, a patio, and a sliver of yard home. They are on friendly terms with a kennel. Even though they are old dogs, they have learned new tricks: not to bark at every truck, car, person, and dog that comes down the street. They know that when we walk down the alleys they don't have to heel, but on the sidewalk they do. They live mostly indoors now and happily greet visitors, many of whom are new friends. Well, Digs does. Lila still thinks you should choose your friends carefully.

I have learned new tricks too. Not only have I become highly skilled at picking up dog poop, but I have also learned how to be loved.

It was love that gave me the vegetable garden. The love of a neighbor and the love of a man. Both organic.

My neighbor and old friend Babs used to own the lot and house. We go way back; we were in the same cooperative day-care center in the 1970s. She and her husband, Ronn, were pre-hippie beatniks. Both artists and intellectuals who never backed down from what they thought was righteous. They were part of the hip backbone of Bloomington, instigators of the city's artists' co-op and founders of Bloomington's first natural foods store, the Clear Moment (named after the clear moment Ronn had when he realized that eating health food may lead to more and more clear moments). He was a fierce organic gardener.

But times change. Ronn died. Babs sold the house and moved to Indianapolis. And my ummm-friend, Steve, bought it.

You know ummm-friend. What you say when you introduce your lover to your family. "This is Steve, my, ummm, friend."

He rents out the house to garden-challenged grad students and, knowing I missed the glory of a veggie plot, offered the rich backyard to me.

*　　*　　*

Later that evening I logged on to Facebook to cruise through the newsfeed. On the dirt photo I'd posted, Babs and I were doing a fast back-and-forth about the garden, chemical-free for twenty years, she noted.

"I can feel Ronn in the soil," I commented.

"That's because he really *is* there," she replied. His ashes, from ten years ago.

"Makes me think of the homegrown tomato song," Steve piped in.

That's one of the things I love about him: he injects what I would never think of. It's the last stanza of Guy Clark's 1983 song, "Homegrown Tomatoes":

When I die don't bury me
In a box in a cemetery
Out in the garden would be much better
I could be pushin' up homegrown tomatoes

We first met at a party right after I moved to town. No sparks flew. I wasn't even sure I liked Steve, or he me. I thought he was too bitter about his divorce. Besides, I was over men; I didn't need to date. I was perfectly fine, and I mean *perfectly* fine, with no lover in my life.

But we persisted in each other's world, stumbling onto each other often at the Bloomingfoods co-op or in the neighborhood. His easygoing smile made me feel strangely nervous, but our conversations kept getting better.

We played shuffle for three years:

He was dating an old friend of mine, they broke up.

We danced together at a bar, a couple times.

I decided again that I wasn't dating.

I unfriended him on Facebook.

Steve got a new girlfriend.

They broke up.

I met a guy who seemed interesting and I tried dating again, just about the time that Steve texted me after we saw each other at Bloomingfoods: "It's always a treat to bump into you out and about . . . how about dinner sometime . . . no expectations."

Alas. "We are out of sync," I texted him back.

"Timing is everything," he replied.

"It's one thing," I texted back.

A couple weeks later I broke it off with the guy I had been seeing (this one lasted the longest of anyone yet, a full forty-nine days). It had been just too much trouble, made me feel crowded. I was in retreat to my comfy non-dating stance when I paused in a moment of uncertainty. It felt like this thing with Steve needed to be settled.

There was something about him; he kept showing up. Maybe a door was open that I should walk through.

"Do I want a relationship?" I asked myself in my journal.

"Well, if it's not too much of a bother," I answered.

"What are your core beliefs about relationships?" I asked myself. Then, as usual, I made a list:

1. I am not lovable.
2. I can't handle conflict.
3. I am safe and happy now. If I'm in a relationship, I'll lose control and put myself at risk. But I'd do it if it were more fun than bad.

So I texted Steve. Told him I'd broken things off, writing, "Our needs were just too different."

And in his big-bite style, he replied, "Oh, those needs. Want to go out tonight?"

It was easy.

Remarkably, he's not afraid to love me. The first time Steve said he loved me, I asked him if it was safe. "No," he said in the dark on the other side of the bed, "but I can't help it."

I stayed awake all night worrying about it. And then I decided to crack open the hard hull of my heart. To no longer believe that I was not lovable.

I think we used those three shuffle years to get our sequences and intersections aligned. To get our heads in the right places, to experience everything we needed to experience so that we could appreciate what we have. It took us almost our whole lives to be ready for each other. It's the hallmark of geezer new love.

But, surprise, surprise, it's not a traditional relationship.

We keep separate households – me in town, him in the woods. We have no plans to live together or marry. It would be so complicated and so unnecessary. Besides, we like the open spaces between us just as much as we like being close. We don't complete each other; we expand each other.

I've learned that we are part of the newest trend in relationships, hip, even, and increasingly common, especially in big cities. We belong to the emerging LAT (Living Apart Together) demographic. It's considered a new family form. Committed couples who live separately. Intimacy and autonomy paired well like steak and wine.

It's still easy after more than a year. Lila even likes him.

Mostly I've quit counting the number of days, even months. Now I'm on years. You never know, because things, well, they change, but we might have twenty years, taking us into our eighties. If we're really lucky, we'll get thirty.

We like to say we're lucky.

Notes

2. SURVIVOR

The lyrics are from Cyndi Lauper's "Time After Time," *She's So Unusual,* Portrait Records, 1983.

3. WATERLOO

"Waterloo" is from a single by Stonewall Jackson, *Waterloo,* Columbia Records, 1959.

6. LINE OF SALT

The gardening-catalog description is of "Little Honey," Oakleaf Hydrangea Bush, Hirt's Gardens, http://www.hirts.com/Little-Honey-Oakleaf-Hydrangea -Bush/dp/B000OCQ67K.

At first I thought the poem "Don't Wait" was written by my grandfather, but further research showed that it was not. As an anonymous poem with various titles (including "When I Quit," "Living Bouquets," and "Don't"), it frequents funeral remembrances still today.

8. CONSILIENCE

For Gwyneth Paltrow's speech see *Proof,* directed by John Madden, 2005; Miramax Films, DVD, 2006.

The E.O. Wilson quotes are from *Consilience: The Unity of Knowledge* (New York: Alfred A. Knopf, 1998). The quote on rational thought is from page 113; the quote on choice and the legacy of the Enlightenment is from page 297.

11. THE IN BETWEEN

Mary Oliver's poem, "Just a Minute," is from *Why I Wake Early: New Poems* (Boston: Beacon Press, 2004).

The song-circle chant is Libana's, "River of Birds," *A Circle Is Cast,* 1986; Spinning Records, CD, 2002.

For the essay on "the void in between," see Danaan Parry, "The Fear of Transformation," *Essene Book of Days* (Santa Fe, NM: Sunstone Press, 1994).

14. FUMES

For information on pheromones, see "Pheromone," *Wikipedia,* http://en .wikipedia.org/w/index.php?title=Pheromone&oldid=617908996; John W. Kimball, ed., "Pheromones," *Kimball's Biology Pages,* http://users.rcn.com/jkimball .ma.ultranet/BiologyPages/P/Pheromones.html; "Communication in Dogs, ACS Distance Education, http://www.acsedu.com/info/pets/animal-care-and -handling/dog-communication.aspx; and Kirk Anderson, "No Place to Run, No Place to Hide: Acacia Defense," GardenSMART, http://www.gardensmart .com/?p=articles&title=Acacia_Defense_Living_Desert.

On the nasogenital alliance, see D. Michael Stoddart, "Follow Your Nose," review of *Smell the Secret Seducer* by Piet Vroon, *New York Times* Book Review online, May 9, 2005, http://www.nytimes.com/books/97/09/28/reviews/970928 .28stoddat.html; Nicholas Wade, "Gay Men Are Found to Have Different Scent of Attraction," *New York Times,* http://www.nytimes.com/2005/05/09/science /09cnd-smell.html?pagewanted=all&_r=0.

The Player's Pub music is Carlyn Lindsey and Snake Doctor, "Maybe I Should Follow You Home," *Live at Players Pub,* Timothy L. Haas/Carlyn Lindsey and SnakeDoctor, CD, 2007.

15. FINDING BOXERWOOD

Boxerwood's mission statement has changed since 2007. It is now "to educate and inspire people of all ages to become effective stewards of the earth." Boxerwood Nature Center and Woodland Garden, Boxerwood Education Association, http://boxerwood.org/aboutus/index.asp.

16. CRABBOTTOM GRITS

On the Arbogasts and the Shawnee massacre see William T. Price, *Historical Sketches of Pocahontas County, West Virginia* (Westminster, MD: Heritage Books, 2008), 123.

For the quote on the Soul Trader's descriptions of America, see Friedrich Bente, *American Lutheranism* (St. Louis: Concordia Publishing House, 1919), 1:51.

18. SIX YEARS LATER

Guy Clark, "Homegrown Tomatoes," *Better Days,* Warner Brothers, LP, 1983.

Book Club Guide

1. In the first chapter of *Leave the Dogs at Home,* it says that Claire and Jim "were the most unlikely of lovers" and that "a mystical gold cord . . . linked us solar plexus to solar plexus." **Do you think Jim thought there was a gold cord linking them or was that something that was there only for Claire? What do you think of the relationship of Claire and Jim? Why did Claire like him? How would you describe Jim? What are the different ways Claire views Jim? Why did the relationship continue over the years? What was good about it? What kind of experience do you have with difficult, complicated love?**

2. Claire fills the hole that Jim left with friendships and interests in the larger world. In the chapter "Fumes" she writes, "Jim's gift to me, the freedom to find another life, was bigger than just plugging in some other kind of guy." **Were you disappointed or happy that Claire fell in love again in the last chapter and why?**

3. **What is the influence of popular culture (television, movies, books, poetry, advertising, music, magazines, dating services, etc.) on our expectations of romance, love, and partnerships? How are people who are not in relationships stereotyped, stigmatized, and discriminated against – at**

work, financially (from two for one coupons to taxes), and socially? What is the view of relationships and marriage in *Leave the Dogs at Home*?

4. Jim and Claire's relationship changes from independent to dependent during the course of Jim's illness. **What were the forces that stimulated the shift?**

5. There are many places in the book where Claire admits to lying. **Do you think she is a reliable storyteller or does her confession of lying make her seem less honest? If so, why? How can a confessed liar seem honest? What role does lying have in relationships with romantic partners, coworkers, and friends?**

6. Many times in the book Claire deludes herself by ignoring key information or zeroing in on just what she wants to hear or see. **What does that tell you about her?**

7. **What types of personal growth does Claire experience? What obstacles does she have to overcome? What did you learn from the ways she grew and changed? What did she do or think that made you feel uncomfortable or made you laugh? Does Claire leave the In Between?**

8. **What role do the dogs play in Claire's journey from feeling broken to having a better life? How do the personalities of the dogs (Lila the sweet but cautious, Diggity the outgoing but broken-hearted) interact and help Claire? Why is the book titled *Leave the Dogs at Home*?**

9. Claire describes her gardens throughout the book and her visit to Boxerwood Gardens is a pivotal moment. **What do these gardens suggest about the way Claire sees the world? Why did Boxerwood have such an impact? Many feel gardening is therapeutic: Why? In what way does the language of the book connect emotion to nature? What role do gardens have in our society?**

10. **How do Claire's travels change her?**

11. **How do roots and family histories operate in the story? What role did Emily, Claire's daughter, play?**

12. Throughout the book, Claire is a list maker and lover of details. **What does that tell you about her, and how does that help or hinder her development?**

13. Toward the end of the book Claire revises the seven stages of grief. **How do traditions surrounding grief influence Claire? Why does the clinically dismissed stages of grief model continue to predominate in grief materials? In what ways is** *Leave the Dogs at Home* **uplifting despite the grief and loss at the center of the story?**

14. **What is changed by Claire's move into town? How do places, houses, and architecture influence the story?**

CLAIRE S. ARBOGAST grew up among the winding streets and deep front porches of historic Irvington on the east side of Indianapolis. She started out as a kid who loved to curl up in hidden places with books and pick gooseberries with her grandmother for tart, bubbling pies. Her family owned flower shops and had a fondness for picnics in state parks. She has planted scores of gardens, some fruitful and stunning, others bratty failures, and has left behind a long line of peony bushes surely still blooming every spring.

Claire now gardens, walks with dogs, and writes in Bloomington, Indiana, and relishes every sweet day. She's in a thoroughly modern LAT relationship (living apart, together) with her honey, Steve, and watches with keen interest as her daughter, Emily, forges her own path through the world.

But what's really important is that Claire has been forever experimenting with life, first as a war protester, then as a tune-in/drop-out hippie. A short marriage, then a single mom. Seven communes in all and a stint deep in the Alaskan woods created a fierce drive for self-determination instead of reliance on others, leading to college and a marketing career. Now she's a writer and local-issue incrementalist who campaigns for brown rice on the hot bar and improved drains at the end of the street. Claire's website is www.ClaireArbogast.com.

Lightning Source UK Ltd.
Milton Keynes UK
UKOW02f0938180815

257110UK00003B/55/P